Jesus Christ Is With Us

Jesus Christ Is With Us:
A Theology in Celebration
of the Indwelling Christ

By Kenneth L. Thrasher

WIPF & STOCK · Eugene, Oregon

Wipf and Stock Publishers
199 W 8th Ave, Suite 3
Eugene, OR 97401

Jesus Christ Is With Us
By Thrasher, Kenneth L.
Copyright©1983 by Thrasher, Kenneth L.
ISBN 13: 978-1-60899-780-0
Publication date 6/25/2010
Previously published by DaySpring Press, 1983

Dedication:
To
Judy,
Karl,
and Amy,
whose interest in this work
has remained steadfast
and whose encouragement
was indispensible
in bringing this volume into
existence, and to my parents,
Luther L. Thrasher and
Exie Kennedy Thrasher.

Preface

With a great sense of celebration and joyous privilege, I send this little volume forth. The indwelling of Christ has not been presented in a complete monogram in many years and surely it is time that the Christian community have such a treatment of this essential reality of its experience in a contemporary interpretation. This is the main theme of *Jesus Christ Is With Us*. This main theme, however, immediately implies and activates another great related theme which has likewise been strangely subordinated, almost to the point of obliteration — that of the *Logos* interpretation of Christ as presented in John 1:1-18. I am advocating the recovery of these two powerful, vital themes in Christian teaching, but more than that, their utilization in Christian experience, of which they are the only source.

If our suspicion of mysticism, sometimes well-grounded, has been the cause of Christian neglect of the indwelling of Christ, it is time to put such suspicion aside by invoking the glorious freedom of the sons of God which his indwelling provides. If our suspicion of all philosophy and metaphysics, again perhaps on good ground for there is much bad philosophy and bad metaphysics, has been the cause of our losing the grand vision of Christ as the Eternal *Logos* (Word) of God who performed indispensible ministries *before* he became flesh and dwelt among us, then we must seize the liberation provided by the fact that "we have the mind of Christ" (I Corinthians 2:16).

I make no apology for the lyrical mode in which this work is cast. My earnest desire is to write theology that could be set to music. My aim is to inspire the Christian to trust Christ more completely and to live his victory as well as to provide the yet unconvinced with a nontechnical apologetic based on Christian experience. I place this volume in your hands as a part of my obedience to the command of the Lord given to the demoniac of Gadara and through him to us all who name the name above every name: "…tell them how great things the Lord hath done for thee, and hath had compassion on thee" (Mark 5:19b).

Kenneth L. Thrasher

Contents

Chapter 1 - The Promise and the Presence 1

Chapter 2 - The Gospel Accompanied by
the Spirit 18

Chapter 3 - Together in Heavenly Places 31

Chapter 4 - The Capacity to Contain
the Divine Presence 44

Chapter 5 - God Through All and
God in You All 57

Chapter 6 - The Eternal Word Steps Forth 71

Chapter 7 - The Cross and
the Atoning Sacrifice 77

Chapter 8 - The Victor From
the Dark Domain 87

Chapter 9 - The Metaphysic of Consecration 95

CHAPTER 1

The Promise and the Presence

Among the many "great and precious promises" Jesus made to his disciples, the most glorious was that he would continue to be with them. This promise would have been properly considered quite absurd by his little band of twelve, as well as by ourselves, had it not been for a wonderful new situation that had just developed — the one who had promised this had been undeniably dead but was now indisputably alive! This fact could scarcely escape the notice of the blindest men in Jerusalem! It could command the undivided attention of the most suspicious and cynical in the crowd!

JESUS CHRIST WAS WITH THEM AND WITH US

They had no doubt that Jesus had been dead. With horror they had watched as he was being murdered. After hours of agony on the Cross, he had finally surrendered his life. And he was dead, truly dead. But not, however, with just the common form of death which is at the end of every ordinary human life. Jesus' death was so much more than that! — it had been designated by the Heavenly Father to destroy the last enemy itself.

In deep despair his disciples sought him among the dead, but he could not be found. They looked for him in the tomb, but he was not there. Death, it developed, could not hold him; the grave, it became evident, could not contain him. And now he presented himself alive! But not, however, with just the same kind of life he had lived with them in the flesh; not with a mere restoration of the common human life he had enjoyed so much and elevated to such hallowed heights. Rather, Jesus was alive with a totally new kind of life! Radiant with a strange new glory, unlike poor Lazarus who must face the grave again, Jesus did not return to life on *this* side of death. He passed through, coming out on the *other* side. In doing so, he opened the grave as if it were a door through which those who trusted in him would enter the heavenly realm to receive their eternal life, being kept for them as an inheritance, described by the Apostle Peter as absolutely secure, "incorruptible," "undefiled," and unfading (I Peter 1:4).

Three days after he had tasted death for every person, Jesus stepped swiftly into his disciples' lives again. With his newly won status as the "victor from the dark domain," he came quickly to them. He wanted to rescue them from their disappointment and the terrible desolation they felt after Calvary.

So now the one who had been crucified, the one who had been so vainly sought in the graveyard, stood before them announcing with the greatest confidence:

> All authority in heaven and on earth has been given to me. Go therefore and make disciples of all nations, baptizing them in the name of the Father and of the Son and of the Holy Spirit, teaching them to observe all that I have commanded you; and lo, I am with you always, to the close of the age.
>
> (Matthew 28:18b-20 RSV)

The Promise and the Presence

Jesus stood before them in a new kind of reality, one which had never been known before in either earth or heaven. The new reality was just this — resurrection life! No resurrected person had ever before set foot upon the cobble stones of the streets of David's city or even upon those golden streets of the new Jerusalem, the heavenly city John would later see coming down. As the Risen One, Jesus opened for them and for us totally new dimensions of existence and offered to all previously inconceivable spiritual power.

As he stood there in his shining newness, in his resurrection glory, he was bringing into their experience, as he would bring into ours, the matchless miracle of God's lovingkindness and redeeming grace. In being called from the cold confines of the tomb in Joseph of Arimathaea's Garden, Jesus had brought to its highest conclusion that stream of God's redemptive intervention into our affairs which began with the calling of Abraham. This saving history reached its climax when God none too gently pushed the stone away from Jesus' mausoleum and summoned him to resurrected life.

In his resurrection glory, he was truly the Eternal in their very midst; he was God's salvation walking down the road with them and joining their various gatherings. He was the window of heaven which God had opened through which came cascades of light and life. With unhindered ease and a certainty as silent as the wind, the presence of the Lord was flowing into this very world, flooding the little broken cisterns of their lives with more spirit and power than they ever dreamed possible.

This is how it was three days after he was taken down from the Cross — the apparent victim had become the victor! Jesus was with his disciples and in that presence they rejoiced! "Lo, I am with you always, even to the end of the world" — this is the promise he was now keeping. And what a glorious thing it was to them and to us!

Had Jesus made this promise, however, merely as the Man of Nazareth and Carpenter of Galilee, it would have been truly an absurd promise and the hopes of his people would certainly have been tragically dashed. But he was more than Nazareth man, more than Galilean carpenter. He was the Eternal Son and word of God who had become flesh to dwell among them.

Without his status as the Eternal Son, the *Logos* of God, his death, though heroic and full of pathos, would have been no more to us than the death of Socrates. Without his status as the *Logos*, his resurrection would have been only a resuscitation to human life still on this side of death. There would have been no redemption and we would still be in the bondage of sin and death. Without his real and true victory over these voracious intruders to set the capstone of his historical sojourn in the world, Jesus could not be with us now. Without this victory, he could not have promised to be with us in any way other than Socrates, Martin Luther, Abraham Lincoln or any other historical figure could have promised to be. And he could not have had such victory if he were only a man, however good and truly man he might have been. To do what he did, he must be Immanuel, God with us. So he was. The *Logos* became flesh and dwelt among us for a short but momentous span of years.

But had Jesus not also been the Man of Nazareth and Carpenter of Galilee, his promise would have been equally without the possibility of fulfillment. If Jesus had not been really "there," he could not be with us "here." If there were not this specific, particular "then," there could not be a contemporary "now" for us in which he indwells believing hearts.

But since he was there with Peter, James and John, Caiaphas, Pilate and Herod, the Samaritan woman, the demoniac dwelling among the tombs, and the invalid for thirty-nine years by the pool of Bethesda, and all the rest of the people of his day whom he encountered in his historical existence, he can be with us here and now in these days so far away from his own in time and place. He is with us now in spiritual communion as our eternal contemporary.

Since he was and is the son of glory, the only begotten of the Father, the word of God who became flesh and lived with us, subsequently bore his cross in the most excruciating agony, then arose in victory breaking the bonds of sin and death, he can be with us in a new and living way. Without these trophies in hand, he could not have been with them and us in no other way than could Socrates or Martin Luther or any other historical figure.

Yet other great historical figures are with us. Socrates *is* with us. Martin Luther *is* with us. Abraham Lincoln *is* with us. Departed loved ones, absent friends, the heroes and villains of childhood memories all are with us. But Jesus Christ is with us like no other can ever be.

This man Socrates, the most influential figure in ancient Greece is with us in many ways. In the example of his courage in the face of death, in showing us that the principles by which one lives are more important than life inself — he is with us. Refusing to give up his convictions, he calmly drank the poisonous hemlock administered by those in power whose superficial morality he had outraged. Socrates is with us.

And Martin Luther is with us. He continues to live through the power of the Protestant Reformation. He is with us in his theological writings and his glorious hymn — "A mighty fortress is our God, A bulwark never failing; Our helper He, amid the flood of mortal ills prevailing." Set to incomparable music, these words become the manifesto of Reformation victory.

At the Diet of Worms, when he was commanded to retract some impassioned claims and convictional affirmations he had made, Luther stood within the Mighty Fortress about whom he had written and in whose security he had come to live and replied with deep serenity of soul, though he trembled on the surface: "I cannot, I will not recant. Here I stand. I cannot do otherwise. God help me." In so replying, Martin Luther set in motion forces that swept into being a new era of the adventure of the human spirit. So Martin Luther is with us.

Abraham Lincoln is with us. As the most excellent embodiment of the American ideal, as the martyred hero of a moral cause, Abraham Lincoln is with us. Through the spiritual aesthetic of his Gettysburg Address, his accomplishments in our highest office and his brooding image upon the still banks of the Potomac, Abraham Lincoln is with us.

Great historical personages are with us through our memory of them, their biographies and teachings. Some are with us through their philanthropies, legislation they enact, institutions and ideas they leave behind. But this is a fragile presence based upon historical artifacts and subject to erosion which marks the shifting sands of human memory and favor.

However, when Jesus said, "Lo, I am with you always, even to the end of the world," he spoke of a presence totally different from that possible to any other historical figure. He is with us in a new and living way since his redemptive death and resurrection. This is the presence he gives to us by dwelling in our hearts through faith. It is a presence which changes life, eradicates sin, provides the power for victorious overcoming, and issues forth in unfathomable joy and peace that passes human understanding. This is his presence which is redemptive and saving. It makes us Christian by its very coming.

This presence depends upon his victory over death, his triumph over the grave — his defeat of the powers and principalities on Calvary's hill and in Joseph of Arimathaea's garden. It depends upon his present intercession as a high priest who ever lives to make intercession for us and upon "the power of an endless life" (Hebrews 7:16), involving the most amazing dynamics of heaven and earth, eternity and time. It hinges upon the reality of the word who became flesh and dwelt among us. This presence is given only to those who, as Jesus required in his first reported sermon, "repent and believe the gospel" (Mark 1:15).

Those who rejoice in this redeeming presence of Jesus reach to him as he walks with them along life's way. They call to him from the darkness of tragedy and suffering and receive his consolation. They hear his still small voice speaking calm and courage in their own sometimes fearful depths. That perfect glow of burning love gives them the power to triumph over death and over life, to stand against powers and principalities as they move along their pilgrimmage to that city whose builder and maker is God.

Jesus' presence through faith makes all the difference in the world in our lives. It is the greatest source of power for overcoming, the unending spring of encouragement in the face of disaster and disintegration, and the never failing ramparts of victory in the face of sin and death. The warm, loving, personal presence of Jesus Christ himself is with us when we allow him to reside within through faith and believing trust. I am with you even to the end of your world and of the world itself is his promise.

There are so many occasions when Jesus takes the initiative to make us aware of his presence with us. He delights in assuring us again and again that he is keeping his promise. On every revelation of this, our hearts sing and rejoice.

PENTECOST AND THE INWARD MOVE

Jesus' disciples were so amazed at his post-Resurrection appearances to them that they could not realize there was another momentous step to be taken, a gigantic move to be made. With the experience of Pentecost, his presence would become inward and permanent. Up to this point, his appearances had been *to* them. He was still external to them, still outside their lives and his presence was like the presence of any other person — sometimes he was at hand, sometimes he was not there. But the next scheduled event in the drama of God's salvation would change all that!

It was a very far-reaching promise Jesus made when he promised to send the Comforter to them. Little did his disciples grasp the magnitude of what the coming of the Holy Spirit would mean. But Jesus had made the promise very lucid:

> ...ye shall receive power, after that the Holy Ghost is come upon you: and ye shall be witnesses unto me both in Jerusalem, and in all Judaea, and in Samaria, and unto the uttermost part of the earth (Acts 1:8 KJV).

Just a few days after his triumph over sin and death through the Cross and Resurrection, Jesus would send the Comforter. Through the fulfillment of this promise, he would be with them to the ends of the world and for the rest of the ages.

They did not know; they could not imagine what the giving of the Comforter would mean to them, nor could

The Promise and the Presence

they conceive the fantastic change his coming would bring about in the structure of their relationship with Jesus himself. Their eyes had not seen, their ears had not heard, neither had the scope of this blessing been conceived in their hearts, but this is what it meant — Jesus himself would take up residence within them! Moving from the outside to the interior, the risen Jesus Christ would dwell in their hearts!

This movement of Christ from the outside of them into their inner life is exactly what occurred at Pentecost (Acts 2). The outpouring of the Holy Spirit was, in fact, an inpouring. It was this: the external Jesus became the internal companion and resident Savior. He became at that moment the indwelling Lord just as he had said again and again that he would. He had said it so specifically:

> If a man love me, he will keep my words: and my Father will love him, and we will come unto him, and make our abode with him (John 14:23 KJV).

> I in them, and thou in me...(John 17:23).

> Abide in me, and I in you...I am the vine, ye are the branches: He that abideth in me, and I in him, the same bringeth forth much fruit...If ye abide in me, and my words abide in you, ye shall ask what ye will, and it shall be done unto you (John 15:4,5,7 KJV).

> And I will pray the Father, and he shall give you another Comforter, that he may abide with you forever: Even the Spirit of truth: whom the world cannot receive, because it seeth him not, neither knoweth him: but ye know him for he dwelleth with you, and shall be in you.
> (John 14:16-17 KJV)

The Spirit was *with* them at the moment when Jesus spoke ("he dwelleth with you"), but he would be *in* them ("and shall be *in* you"). Jesus said many other words to this same effect — that he abides in the Father, the Father abides in him, and that both Father and Son will abide in all Christians by means of the Holy Spirit.

Now it was done — like a mighty rushing wind the Spirit came and in his coming Jesus Christ was alive in their hearts. He had moved inside. No longer would they have to look for his appearing in Upper Rooms or on Roads to some distant Emmaus. No longer would they have to search for him in any external form or place where he might be mistaken for the gardener again. He would now be closer to them, and to us, than they could ever be even to themselves.

The Holy Spirit, of course, had never been absent. He had been with Jesus from the beginning. Conceived by the Holy Spirit and the Virgin Mary, authenticated as the Eternal Beloved Son by the Holy Spirit at his baptism, upheld and lead by the Spirit throughout his ministry, Jesus knew him well for he (the Spirit) descended and remained on him (John 1:33). Not only during his earthly sojourn, but also in the endless reaches of eternity they had been acquainted. The Godhead had always been Father, Son and Holy Spirit — God in three persons unto which blessed Trinity we rightly sing, "Holy, Holy, Holy," just as cherubim and seraphim had done. "Remaining on him" (John 1:33) for the rest of his earthly life, this Holy Spirit would be given to them and to us at the set time. From Pentecost onward, the holy presence would be *within* the redeemed human heart.

At the fulfillment of the Pentecost promise, not only did all believers receive the indwelling of Christ as the strength from which all spiritual power flows, but also Jesus was given his full recognition as "both Lord and Christ." Peter, proclaiming with irresistable force, said,

This Jesus hath God raised up, whereof we all are witnesses. Therefore being by the right hand of God exalted, and having received of the Father the promise of the Holy Ghost, he hath shed forth this, which ye now see and hear. Therefore, let all the house of Israel know assuredly, that God hath made that same Jesus, whom ye have crucified, both Lord and Christ.

(Acts 2:32-33,36 KJV)

Having been born of woman, born under the law, having triumphed over sin and death on the Cross and in the Resurrection, having been exalted to the right hand of the Father and declared to be "both Lord and Christ," now at Pentecost in a great display of spiritual power Jesus Christ, once humiliated now exalted, takes up his residence in the hearts of all who had believed in him.

"THE PROMISE IS UNTO YOU AND TO YOUR CHILDREN" (Acts 2:39)

And gloriously the promise and its fulfillment was not just to these original disciples. It was to us all! In the latter days of Rome's grandeur, the living Christ dwelt in the hearts of those outlawed ones who, in the face of impending brutal death, could scratch in the stone of catacomb walls the affirmation of life — Vita, Vita, Vita! "Life, life, life," they proclaimed, because Jesus Christ was alive in them!

In the dark Middle Ages, the serf in his hovel who had heard the good news of Christ, repented and believed it, had a living light within him which no worldly darkness, no earthly lord or fiend from hell could quench. This indwelling presence of Christ was and is for all who would hear and accept the invitation, "Come unto me all ye that labor and are heavy laden, and I will give you rest" (Matthew 11:28).

What glory there was in the missionary promise as the gospel went out from European shores as the occasion to celebrate the indwelling wonder was shared with distant tribes and nations. Lowell Mason's great hymn catches the heroism of the gospel's proclamation:

> From Greenland's icy mountains, From India's coral strand, Where Africa's sunny fountains, Roll down their golden sand, From many an ancient river, From many a palmy plain, They call us to deliver, Their land from error's chain.
>
> ("From Greenland's Icy Mountains," *Baptist Hymnal*, 1956, p. 449)

Their deliverance would come, and did come, like ours, by the indwelling of the victorious Lord and Christ, Jesus of Nazareth and Eternal word of God, who had triumphed by the blood of his Cross and the opening of his grave with Resurrection power.

When *anyone* takes Jesus Christ as Lord and Savior through repentance and faith, he moves into the believing heart to take up permanent residence within that person's life. When we take him as Savior and he begins immediately to dwell within us, every aspect of our life is changed. The difference is so great that we must proclaim the transformation a miracle.

To our physical birth, he adds a spiritual birth.

To our earthly life, he adds the life eternal.

To the old creation given to us by God at the beginning, he adds a new creation which brings the old to its proper fulfillment.

To our sinful past, marked with death and darkness, saturated with sin, there is added a cleansed and eternal future in which forgiveness and love reign supreme through Christ's indwelling.

To our broken rationality, he adds that quality which justifies our saying, "...we have the mind of Christ" (I Corinthians 2:16).

The Promise and the Presence

To the clanging cymbals of a hollow life, he adds meaningful spiritual depths.

To the solitary dialogue we carry on within ourselves, he adds his eternal voice revealing God's will for us by illuminating our minds to understand the Scripture.

To our solitary walk through the times and places of life, he draws near and adds a heavenly companionship which makes hard times victorious and the rough places plain (Isaiah 40:4).

From our lowly places from the ends of the earth, we are lifted up and made to sit together in heavenly places in Christ Jesus (Ephesians 2:6).

And finally, we shall be found among those who appear in John's vision: "...I saw the dead, small and great, stand before God" (Revelation 20:12a). We shall hear the Lord say, "Come, ye blessed of my Father, inherit the kingdom prepared for you from the foundation of the world" (Matthew 25:34b). All these things are our portion and heritage because the indwelling of Christ has added immortality and life to our fragile frames. "The Spirit itself beareth witness with our spirit, that we are the children of God" (Romans 8:16).

It is necessary, therefore, that Christ actually be alive in us if we are to have this hope of glory. As William Law said, "A Christ not in us is a Christ not ours." All these benefits and blessings of Christ accrue to us from within, from him who is in vital union with our spirits. Without this union with him, we have not accepted him as our Lord and we are still "...aliens from the commonwealth of Israel, and strangers from the covenants of promise, having no hope, and without God in the world:" (Ephesians 2:12).

If Christ is still outside us, he demands to know why we have refused to be included in his saving grace manifested on the Cross. He demands to know why we have refused his loving invitation to come unto him. If Christ is still outside us, he is in travail with loving pathos for us until we allow him to be the new creation in us. Dead in trespasses and sins, we stand outside him. Unforgiven and unredeemed, we stand along side him. Standing outside him, standing along side him, we know him only as both prosecutor and judge. Inside us, he is our loving Savior and Lord who bore our griefs and carried our sorrow. Christ himself is in grief for everyone to whom he is external. This grief in the divine life continues "...until Christ be formed in you" (Galatians 4:19b). So it is "Christ *in you*" and *only* in you who is "the hope of glory" (Colossians 1:27).

Through faith in Christ, the "fullness of the Godhead bodily" (Colossians 2:9) — Father, Son and Holy Spirit, comes to dwell in us. When we have Christ, we have God since "it pleased the Father that in him should all the fullness dwell" (Colossians 1:19). When Christ is in us, the Father is in us and the Holy Spirit is in us.

The great fact of Christ's indwelling is the Apostle Paul's greatest joy! It is everything to him. He celebrates it, affirms it, proclaims it, in some of the grandest verses in the New Testament.

"For me to live is Christ (Philippians 1:21).

"I live, and yet no longer I, but Christ liveth in me" (Galatians 2:20).

"Know ye not that ye are the temple of God, and that the Spirit of God dwelleth in you?" (I Corinthians 3:16).

"But ye are not in the flesh, but in the Spirit, if so be that the Spirit of God dwell in you. Know if any man have not the Spirit of Christ, he is none of his. And if Christ be in you, the body is dead because of sin; but the Spirit is life because of righteousness. But if the Spirit of him that raised up Jesus from the dead shall also quicken your mortal bodies by his Spirit that dwelleth in you" (Romans 8:9-11 KJV).

Christ in you! The Father in you! The Spirit in you! The very fullness of the Godhead dwells bodily in us through Christ. Truly we are awesomely and wonderfully made! Our human heart reflects the glory and genius of its creator in its capacity to contain the living God! This miraculous capability is actualized when Christ is received through faith in the Cross.

Through faith we actually have him alive in us as the tremendous possibilities of the human soul become actual. Without Christ dwelling in the heart, it matters little how much one may have developed various talents, or how diligently self-realization has been cultivated. Regardless of the intensity of such training and cultivation of potential, such a one is radically incomplete. Without Christ in the heart, human life is forever and tragically lacking; the one glory for which it was created is never made its own.

BEING KNIT TOGETHER IN LOVE (Colossians 2:2)

This is the basic truth on which our personal knowledge of Christ as well as our doctrine of Christ must be grounded — that Jesus Christ is a contemporary reality dwelling within us whom we know with convictional certainty in the great diversity of experience we call life. He really keeps that promise. He really lives within our hearts! He reaffirms this over and over — sometimes with the delicate touch of the burning heart as with those on the Emmaus Road. Again, he may reveal himself with an insistent demand to be heard, requiring us to take some rigorous stand for his righteousness' sake. At other times, he may almost overwhelm us, body and soul in exalted spiritual experience as our very being is saturated with his light and joy. Every degree of holy experience, from that of the child who prays, "Now I lay me down to sleep, I pray the Lord my soul to keep," to that of the great Apostle's being caught up in the third heaven, being "caught up into paradise, and heard unspeakable words, which it is not lawful for a man to utter" (II Corinthians 12:4), are all expressions of this truth and examples of this reality. All such experiences great and small are precious reassurances that "he hath said, I will never leave thee, nor forsake thee" (Hebrews 13:5b).

Conscious awareness of this sublime actual indwelling of Christ is the fullest flower of the Christian experience. Realization of the living Lord as our inward and inseparable companion is the capstone of our faith.

The indwelling of Christ is a spiritual unity between the human spirit and the divine spirit. The human personality is a spiritual reality rather than a physical object. And "God is a Spirit..." (John 4:24). Therefore, the Spirit of God can reside in the human spirit and the human spirit can reside in the divine spirit. We are "in Christ" and Christ is in us. This can happen because spiritual realities can interpenetrate one another and can mutually indwell. Two spiritual realities can occupy the same "personal space" without displacing one another or losing their respective identities. "...he who is united to the Lord becomes one spirit with him" (I Corinthians 6:17 RSV).

If we think of spirit as an "energy" or "power" rather than as a "substance," any spatial problem of the indwelling of Christ and our living in him are overcome in advance. Two energies, such as two beams of light, can become one as they approach the same object. They blend into one and yet remain separable. Neither loses its distinctiveness, yet they are at the same time in perfect unity as they occupy the same space while moving toward an object. They do not create a third thing to which both must surrender themselves. They are in a supra-physical unity akin to that of a spiritual unity, each indwelling the other.

Although we can offer no explanation of the mystery of Christ's indwelling of the human spirit just as we cannot explain any other miracle, such examples and instances indicate that there are avenues of explanation which go beyond physical occupancy. Christ is not in us as a physical thing. He is in us as a spiritual power or energy, and our spirit which he indwells is also a spiritual power or energy. Then, his dwelling within us does not destroy our identity. He does not lose his own by dwelling in our spirits. Our spirit and his are intertwined in a mystical union. They mutually inhere as energy to energy or light to light. And since both he and our own inner being are spirit, they can mutually indwell without grotesque results or implications.

The significance of Jesus' being with us and therefore in us has not been fully applied as a principle of interpretation of how wondrously God has made us. The fact that the victorious Christ can and does dwell in our spirits has tremendous implications for the doctrine of man as he emerged from the creator's hand. Nor has the indwelling of Christ been given its full power in our understanding of the Christian life and faith. Yet it is the bedrock truth, the essential ingredient of the experience of all Christians of every age and locality. It is the very source of hope and glory which points to the Author of all life. All these causes for rejoicing are ours because the dayspring from on high which has visited us (Luke 1:78) and is our constant companion which gives us unfailing victory even in such a world as this!

CHAPTER 2

The Gospel Accompanied by the Spirit

Both the actuality of Christ's indwelling and our knowledge of it are brought about through the illumination and application of the biblical word by the Holy Spirit. As Charles H. Spurgeon said, "...the gospel, accompanied by the power of the Spirit, bringeth life" (*Treasury of David*, vol. 1, p. 284).

By his own joyous willingness, the Holy Spirit is committed to accompany the gospel in the world. To the good news of what Jesus Christ has done the Holy Spirit will add his power to illuminate, interpret and apply. Because of the Spirit's work, therefore, the message of the Cross and the Empty Tomb is not just a historical report from the past. It is that and more — it is also a contemporary experience, occurring in the hearts of those who "repent and believe the gospel" (Mark 1:15) as Jesus urged in his first reported sermon.

At the grand climax of the work of Jesus was the privilege which he earned to send the Holy Spirit, the heavenly Comforter and illuminator to all of his disciples. Near the end of his ministry on earth, he spoke often of the promise which he would certainly fulfill. Jesus longed to continue with them forever and his surpassing victory in his redemptive work made it possible for him to do so through the Holy Spirit's ministry. It was the will and delight of the Father as well as of the Holy Spirit himself to so honor the work of Jesus by giving it a living, permanent presence. This would be accomplished through the indwelling of Christ mediated and made operational until the end of the age by the ministry of the Holy Spirit. The fulfillment of the scripture would be the instrument through which this continuing presence would be graciously granted.

THE FULFILLMENT OF SCRIPTURE

Jesus loved the scriptures. For him they consisted solely of the Old Testament. He had saturated his life in the knowledge of them and found in them victory and power. Scriptural words formed his vocabulary. Biblical concepts infused his thought. In the prophet's cries, he cried; in the Psalmist's jubilation, he rejoiced; in David's sorrow, he expressed his sorrow; in the images and figures of Isaiah and Zechariah he conceived and formed his ministry and expressed his life.

One of the most vivid instances of Jesus' understanding of his relation to the scripture is Luke 4:16-21. Here Jesus interprets his life and ministry in terms of Isaiah's prophecy and announced boldly that "this day is this scripture fulfilled in your ears" (v. 21). It was not Jesus' intention, therefore, just to enjoy the Old Testament, or even just to draw strength from it, but rather to perform a major transformation upon it. This transformation consisted of a process which he called "fulfilling" it. The method by which this fulfilling would take place was the bonding of the Holy Spirit's power of interpretation and illumination to the written word in an irrevocable way.

Toward the final act of his life and ministry on earth, Jesus announced to his disciples what the Father intended to do. He told them how the Comforter would be sent and what his role would be. He rejoiced therefore to be able to give them this permanent promise, to inaugurate this process of interaction between the Holy Spirit and the word of his Cross and Resurrection which would continue until the end of the age. He knew that this would give them assurance. He knew this would give them courage — to know that forever more a living power, the Holy Spirit himself would accompany the preaching and witness of his good news mediated through the written word making it a living word in the hearts of hearers. Surely, he greatly rejoiced to tell them this:

> ...the Comforter, which is the Holy Ghost, whom the Father will send in my name, he shall teach you all things, and bring all things to your remembrance, whatsoever I have said unto you (John 14:26 KJV).

When this was accomplished, the gospel would be complete. A living spiritual power would be attached to the words about the Cross and Empty Tomb which would create through the preaching of the Apostles (*kerygma*) and the application of the message to every day life (*didache*) the inspired books we call the New Testament. With the Spirit's never failing illumination, these words would become immeasurably more significant than all the other excellent words of human tongue or pen. The written story of Jesus' redemptive work, both in its actuality and in all the preparatory stages through the prophets and other "men of old" through whom God revealed his intention to save, would become the tool in the hands of the Holy Spirit.

The word of God proper is that word of the Cross and Resurrection in both their actual occurrence and

The Gospel Accompanied by the Spirit

in their historical preparation which in holy freedom the Holy Spirit has permanently embraced as the object of his illumination and interpretation. The Bible, which tells this story of redemption, is itself, therefore, a perpetual wonder, a standing miracle, the never failing source of amazing grace.

Jesus gives an example of this inner voice and power which the Holy Spirit would give to all the scripture. Although in this instance it is Jesus himself who illumines and empowers the scripture, he does so through the Holy Spirit. Afterwards, when he had returned to the Father, the Comforter would continue this work of illumination and teaching as his own major office. The example is contained in Luke 24:27: "And beginning at Moses and all the prophets, he expounded unto them in all the scriptures concerning himself." But the context implies that his disciples did not yet understand what he was saying indicated by their failure to recognize him. At that point, he had not "opened their understanding" (Luke 24:45). That is, he had not given a spiritual voice to those scriptures yet.

Later on, in that same chapter of Luke we read:

> And he said unto them, These are the words which I spoke unto you while I was yet with you, that all things must be fulfilled, which are written in the law of Moses, and in the prophets, and in the psalms, concerning me. *Then he opened their understanding, that they might understand the scriptures* (Luke 24:44-45 KJV).

Once he granted the inner voice to the Old Testament texts, they understood. Their understanding was expressed by their recognition of him.

This instance of opening their understanding was a private experience just for these few disciples on this specific occasion. But it was a foreshadow of the promise which would be extended to everyone after

Pentecost. Jesus had fulfilled the entire Old Testament by being the One of whom it spoke and by accomplishing the work of redemption which was its main intent. And even if Jesus had never uttered a word of it vocally, he "spoke" it with his life and therefore brought it under the promise of John 14:26, including it among those writings which would be living scripture.

The Old Testament must be fulfilled. This was done when Christ's finished work in death and resurrection enabled the Holy Spirit to come to illuminate the written word. When Jesus gave it its inner voice, it found its fulfillment as a spiritual, saving force as the living word of God. This process of illumination is the long awaited fulfillment of the scripture.

THE PRODUCTS OF SPIRIT AND WORD

"The gospel, accompanied by the power of the Spirit" is the means by which all Christian spiritual experience is accomplished. Paramount among these occasions is the power of conviction which sweeps over the assembled congregation at worship. In the preaching, praying, singing and call to commitment, the living Christ is revealed within the worshipping community. "For where two or three are gathered together in my name, there am I in the midst of them" (Matthew 18:20). Being "in the midst" is not an external presence. Christ is within the individual Christian's heart as the pulsating, indwelling spiritual presence which never leaves. But when the congregation is assembled in the oneness of worship in spirit and truth, the diverse members are unified in a corporateness which lifts Christ's presence to an intensity beyond that granted to any individual present and the whole reinforces and strengthens the parts which compose it.

The central activity of this corporate worship is the preaching of the word. The preacher speaks a human word with an earthly voice, but attached to that human word is a divine promise — a promise that the eternal living Spirit will so empower the spoken word of historical witness of the preaching of the Bible, that the eternal saving Word, the Word who was and is Jesus Christ, will step forth into the midst of his waiting people who have gathered in his name. As the gospel is being spoken, the Holy Spirit causes the living Word to step forth. Upon the wings of the written word, Jesus Christ steps forth to reveal himself again to every waiting heart.

In prayer, also, as the soul carries on its deepest communication with God its maker, Jesus Christ through whom we pray becomes very real. He draws near to inspire our prayer, and when our feelings are too intense to be put into words, the Holy Spirit intercedes before the throne for us. He, himself, becomes our prayer as he expresses our desires in groanings that cannot be uttered. We sense the reality of the divine presence in these moments.

In the singing of ancient hymns, the words of the composer become conveyors of our hopes and affirmations, as we feel the living presence of our Lord draw near from within and our souls are drawn to the one of whom we sing.

In the call to commitment which is a part of worship, Jesus Christ is with us. When we are moved toward decision with the pounding of our hearts, terrific stirring of our souls, and the opening of unfathomable deeps of our spirits, then we are sure that he is with us as we take these feelings as sure and certain signs of his loving indwelling. We rejoice in his urging, in his persistent call, in his brooding over us as we sense his forceful, yet gentle, beckoning to us. In the awful conviction of sin which sweeps our souls when our sinfulness is exposed to the holy rays of Calvary's light and love, we know that Jesus Christ is with us.

Jesus is there, actually performing as he promised when he said, "Behold, I stand at the door and knock" (Revelation 3:20). This is a metaphor, of course, referring to the gracious calling of the Lord to us urging that we accept him in order to become Christians.

In this evangelistic phase of worship, the Holy Spirit presents Christ at the door of the heart. Until the door is opened through repentance and faith, however, Christ is still outside. That being the case, we suffer "godly sorrow" because we have not let him in.

We feel this godly sorrow and painful conviction because we know that no person is a Christian until Christ dwells in him. "A Christ not in us is a Christ not ours," said William Law, the eighteenth century author of *A Serious Call to the Devout and Holy Life*. When the heart is finally opened to him, often after a painful period of alternating resistance and resolve to follow Christ, he enters to dwell eternally. This is done when we "repent and believe the gospel" (Mark 1:15). At that moment Jesus Christ comes in to become a permanent resident, bringing the full benefits of his Cross and Resurrection to the life of the repenting and believing one. Then one may affirm that the certainty of Paul's great watchword, "...Christ in you, the hope of glory" (Colossians 1:27b), applies to us as well as the Apostle.

When the door to the heart is opened and Jesus' indwelling becomes a reality, regeneration of life occurs. We are restored to full Sonship with the Father. We are passed from death unto life. Instantly we become new creations in Christ Jesus. What riches of grace await when salvation is accomplished and we become aware that what he said is true: "Behold, I stand at the door and knock." What an invitation to grace we are receiving when we feel his gracious approach.

Christ also stands and knocks on the door of the heart of those who have already received him in saving faith. Of course, Jesus lives in the heart of every Christian. But through sin and neglect, self-will, failure to be obedient and lack of consecration, the Christian may have relegated Christ to an inferior room in his heart, a subordinate place in his soul. Jesus continues therefore to knock on the door of the Christian's heart, but in this case it is a knocking from within. It is the valiant effort of the Lord to move to a higher room, a more prominent place in the heart. Jesus Christ is not satisfied to be subordinate. He will aggressively seek to be the Lord of the life he indwells. His intention is to rule and reign as King. But he can do this only with the consent of the person in whom he dwells. So he continues to knock, asking for the higher place.

"Behold, I stand at the door and knock." For the yet unconverted, the knocking of Christ is on the door of the main entrance. Repentance and faith open it to let him in. For the Christian in whom he already resides, the knocking on the interior doors is his endeavor to gain mastery of the whole house. Fuller surrender to his Lordship, greater consecration to his person, happier acceptance of his will, more complete absorption into his love, — these are the responses one must make to have him seated on the throne of one's life to rule as both Lord and Christ, for he has said, "...if any man will hear my voice and open the door, I will come into him, and sup with him, and he with me" (Revelation 3:20).

In private moments also the Spirit testifies to our spirits that he is with us. In the somber moments of grief as we feel a strong and certain consolation, we know that Jesus Christ is with us.

In times of moral confusion when we know not which way to turn, and then, suddenly, light begins to form within us. Then all the diverse possibilities, all the conflicting alternatives begin to take on a new order and precedence we had been unable to imagine as possible just a moment before. We stop for a moment to render praise and thanksgiving that Jesus Christ is with us.

When, on the road to some perhaps unknown Emmaus, our hearts begin to burn within us and we see light in which we have come to rejoice and sense that presence on which we have come to rely, we know again that Jesus Christ is with us.

When there is a moving of courage and bravery for righteousness' sake which had been absent before, and somebody stands up and exclaims, "I must right this wrong for God's sake!" then Jesus Christ is with us. When people are called on to give themselves in heroic sacrifice to stand up for the weak, or to give cups of cold water in Jesus' name, then and there, Jesus Christ is with us.

In the privacy of our devotions in the quietness of our closet, an undefinable warmth may begin to burn in our hearts. We feel the glorious presence which consoles, convicts and inspires. We feel new assurances of love and grace. We rejoice again at Calvary and the Empty Tomb. This presence bids us, "Peace, be still!" Finding ourselves strangely at one with the eternal, we know the promise is kept. We know that Jesus Christ is with us.

These are the moments, great and small, which change the direction of our lives and the content of our consciousness. These moments send us in new directions, give us courage to stand in the face of sin and death, lead us to committed endeavor for Christ. They are most surely moments when Jesus has kept undeniably his promise, "...lo, I am with you always, even to the end of the world" (Matthew 28:20b).

Jesus is with us as a living spiritual presence, an unseen companion who is all the more visible by his being unseeable, all the more tangible by his being untouchable and all the more audible by his being unheard. This is possible because he is indeed closer to us than we are to ourselves, dwelling within. He has chosen the inner realms of our hearts as his home on earth, continuing his incarnation in us, having made our inner depths his permanent dwelling-place.

Our hearts are God's second home, of course. The one who is in us is also the exalted one above us who inhabits eternity.

> For thus saith the high and lofty One that inhabiteth eternity, whose name is Holy; I dwell in the high and holy place, with him also that is of a contrite and humble spirit...(Isaiah 57:15).

THE QUENCHING OF THE SPIRIT

The direct interaction of the Spirit and scripture is crucial in all spiritual experience. The instrument of the Spirit is the Biblical message, the written word. And although there are many ways to violate the admonition of the Apostle Paul to "Quench not the Spirit" (I Thessalonians 5:19), the most frequent and certain way is to fail to take into one's understanding the written word of God. Notwithstanding the certainty that "Thy word is a lamp unto my feet and a light unto my path" (Psalm 119:105), so many Christians neglect to do as the Psalmist announces that he has done, "Thy word have I hid in mine heart, that I might not sin against thee" (Psalm 119:11). The sin one commits on such failure is not necessarily to be without moral instruction or ethical motives. Rather, it is to be berift of tools the Holy Spirit is committed to using in mediating spiritual resources to us.

Receiving this word through consecrated study of the Bible, our hearts and minds are equipped with instruments the Holy Spirit will use. If our consciousness is permeated by this word of the Lord, then the Holy Spirit freely and certainly uses the word we have assimilated to accomplish his work of mediating the living Word to us. Without knowledge of the Biblical content, the Holy Spirit has no instrument through which to approach us to administer the living presence of Christ. To close one's mind to the Bible is to deny the Holy Spirit entrance into our lives. Then ordinary human feelings and even distorted subjective impulses may be mistakenly identified as the Holy Spirit's revelations and promptings, when, in fact, the Spirit has been quenched by the absence of God's written word in our perceptual mechanism. Ignorance of the written word is the most frequent means by which the Holy Spirit is quenched.

Conversely, saturation of the soul with the written narrative is a certain assurance of the unfailing ministry of the Spirit in us. This written narrative has many forms. It may consist of biographical details of Jesus' life, historical and prophetic preparation for his coming through the history of Israel in the Old Testament, or the exposition of the meaning of Christ's work in the Acts, Epistles and Revelation. But regardless of the part of the narrative under consideration, it becomes the instrument of the Holy Spirit.

The text in preaching or devotional reading, therefore, can be either a simple saying of Jesus, an historical incident from the Old Testament, a Psalm of David, a story of Elijah or Elisha, a phrase, a paragraph from any place in the Bible. It can be a profound theological insight from Paul or a simple saying from Proverbs. As it is related to the saving work of Jesus, it becomes capable of bearing the Holy Spirit's illumination and therefore a vehicle for his ministry to us. When Jesus indicated that the Spirit would call to our remembrance "all that I have said unto you," he meant much more than his own spoken words. They are included in the promise, of course, but since Jesus "spoke" through his actions his full message of salvation, the Spirit is concerned to illumine and teach every word that has to do with that.

The Spirit's ministry is revealing who Jesus is and applying his saving work through the Cross and Resurrection. Therefore, he has blessed the narrative in all its forms which sets forth this saving work. He is committed to the illumination and interpretation of the Biblical story. It is imperative therefore that the story in its diverse forms and expressions, its many stages of development and degrees of completeness be in our perceptual mechanism if the Spirit is to work in our lives. Without the word in us, we have no grounds for expecting to receive the Spirit's ministry. But when the word is rightly hid in our hearts, the Spirit will be there constantly and unfailingly.

To fail to receive the Biblical word either through private study or in public proclamation is ultimately to quench the Spirit and render life dark instead of light, blind instead of seeing, empty rather than full, dreadful rather than joyous.

Throughout this dynamic process of Spirit and word, the Holy Spirit maintains his freedom. As a divine person, he is not mechanically bound by the written word. He has not subjected himself to any system that would allow him to be subjected to human cunning and manipulation. The word is not a tinder-box which requires that he appear when struck a certain number of times. The Spirit always maintains his freedom which is a part of his identity. Jesus states this clearly: "The wind bloweth where it listeth, and thou hearest the sound thereof, but canst not tell whence it cometh, and whither it goeth: so is everyone that is born of the Spirit" (John 3:8).

The divine indwelling comes about through this dynamic interaction between the written story in the Bible and the Holy Spirit. This process goes on within the hearing person, in the heart of the one who hears the witness of the Biblical message. The Bible is the story in external form; the Holy Spirit is the internal voice, the inner light, who interprets and applies the message. Through their interaction these two mediate the indwelling of Christ to the human heart. The word from without, the preached or read gospel, has a living counterpart within the heart. The written story and the living Spirit are inseparable correlates. They are both vital participants in the dynamics through which Christ is encountered from without and from within.

In hearing the gospel again the believers' certainty is confirmed over and over. The conviction that Jesus Christ himself is with us becomes intensively more precious and prized. The deepening commitment of Christ to us makes us know more assuredly that nothing can separate us from his living presence.

CHAPTER 3

Together in Heavenly Places

This common resource of all Christians, this fount of every spiritual blessing, this divine indwelling which is the earnest of redemption, this eternal light given to all who believe, becomes multiform in the practice of the spiritual life. Upon the prism of human individuality it finds expression in a myriad of ways and in numberless variations. Nevertheless, all the essential elements of spiritual experience are the same. Whether the simple warming of the heart, the gentle urge of an emerging conviction, an overwhelming sense of guilt blotted out by grace as expressed in the lines, "Sin had left a crimson stain, He washed it white as snow" (Elvina M. Hall, "Jesus Paid It All," *Baptist Hymnal*, 1975), or a full-orbed mystical experience, the dynamics are always the same — an inner and personal interaction occurring between the indwelling Christ and the personality of the one in whom he dwells. The difference in spiritual experience is one of degree rather than of kind. It is a matter of intensity, rather than of method.

Having spoken of the common and uniform features of Christ's indwelling, we now turn attention to exceptional spiritual experience. Here we find Christ's indwelling expressed in highly individual terms. What we have designated as "exceptional" Christian experience, therefore, becomes highly autobiographical and very personal in the attempt to communicate it to others. The intimacy of the next several pages cannot be avoided and the reader's sympathetic understanding is assumed.

SLAPPED BY AN ANGEL

> And, behold, the angel of the Lord came upon him and a light shined in the prison: and he smote Peter on the side, and raised him up, saying Arise up quickly. And his chains fell off from his hands (Acts 12:7 KJV).

Peter learned that the beginning of a new movement of God is sometimes inaugurated by a quite unexpected shock. In research for his outstanding classic, *The Varieties of Religious Experience*, William James discovered that this sense of being struck was often quite pronounced as the beginning stage of an exceptional spiritual experience. Like a slap on the head or a kick in the side, the presence of the Lord in a special movement may be revealed with shocking forcefulness.

So abrupt is this introductory phrase that one may be seized by a momentary sense of anger and demand to know who struck him. Before such an impertinance can bring forth this action, however, one becomes aware of an exalted feeling within the heart from the very first moment of the process. A strange and powerful process has been initiated in the heart. Instantly one is brought to the realization of a sparkling vitalness, a shimmering but powerful aliveness that has never been known quite this way before. Without a moment's uncertainty the source of this feeling is recognized — it is the Lord!

One knows immediately that this is the beginning of the most glorious experience one would ever know in this earthly life. According to what standard of selection has one been chosen as the theatre for this great divine drama? There is no time for asking. Reflection on what is happening will come later. As for now, one can only exult in the serious joy of the immediacy of the Holy presence.

IMMEDIACY, NATURALNESS AND DOXOLOGY

After the heart is startled into spiritual aliveness, the awareness is instantly occupied with the irradiance of something being formed at the very center of the heart. A vision, to be sure, but not a vision to be seen. Rather it is a vision to be felt. It is at a deeper level than sight. Being enacted within, this vision by-passes the eyes and occurs in the soul.

From the first, one is quite aware of the locale of the occurrence. It is happening in the heart which is now strangely warmed. This phase of what is happening has happened before, but perhaps with less intensity. In worship experiences, in private prayer, in moments of spiritual feeling, this presence has been known in previous but less intense experience. So the Lord is no stranger to us. We know who he is. This is the Comforter Jesus promised to send. In times of religious conviction, such as our conversion to faith in Christ, we have been quite aware of this presence.

We were with him on the Cross. We were there when he rose up from the grave! We died with him! We arose when he did! We have the certainty "...that so many of us as were baptized into Jesus Christ were baptized into his death...Therefore we are buried with him by baptism into his death: that like as Christ was raised up from the dead by the glory of the Father, even so we also should walk in newness of life" (Romans 6:3-4 KJV).

Therefore having shared so deeply with him in his redemptive experience, we do need to ask for identification. Paul's urgent inquiry at his encounter with the Lord on the road to Damascus was, "Who art thou, Lord?" But we do not need to ask. Paul was not yet a Christian when he asked this so urgently. But we know our Savior. Because of our prior acquaintance with him, we are not baffled or confused when such an intense experience arises. It is clearly the Redeemer/King who is with us. It is the one who, though he was rich became poor for our sakes and is now rich again with a new trophy of surpassing wealth resulting from his victory over sin and death.

We are totally captivated by this enacted vision. It is felt with a spiritual faculty that seems to be given in and with the experience itself.

He has unveiled himself immediately in our hearts; we are aware of no instruments he has used. We have not been called on to utilize memory, reason, or emotion. There is no obvious use of scripture verses or songs or any object at the beginning, although later songs of rejoicing and assurances will race through our being. The *immediacy* of his unveiling is strongly evident. It is a one-to-one relationship, a face-to-face encounter with no noticeable intervening devices. Above all, we have not made any effort to bring about this unveiling.

We are impressed with the totally effortless motion by which he has revealed himself. It seems so easy for him. And so "natural." We are so pleased because there is perfect harmony, perfect kinship between ourselves and the Lord. There is no strain; there is no sense of estrangement to be overcome. There is no fear, only unearthly joy! We feel that this moment had always belonged to us as our manifest destiny. How good the love-saturation of our heart feels. So effortless! So appropriate! So totally fitting!

We hear the music of the spheres; we hear the song of the Eternal. It does not sound strange at all! We have heard enough of the rudimentary notes before; we have known the chords that make up this full symphony. Therefore, it is not strange to us.

God is filling our hearts with himself, and we are impressed by the familiarity and naturalness of it all. The cauldrons of the inner deeps are gently bubbling; the waters of our inner Bethesda are delightfully troubled by the heavenly messenger. We do nothing but receive. We had no inkling that we could be this passive! Christ is doing it all.

Charged with all the power and glory of the redemptive sacrifice and resurrection victory, the Lord unveils himself in us and as an accompaniment, he grants us feelings that are simply beyond the power of words to describe. Perhaps the disciples on the Emmaus Road said it about as well as it can be said:

> Did not our heart burn within us, while he talked with us by the way, and while he opened to us the scriptures?
> (Luke 24:32).

While the experience is occurring, however, we are not concerned about words; we are not interested in description. He is so close to us that there is no "room" for reflection or any such concern. Doxology is our only response.

As we are caught up in praise, we find our sense of time has been lost. Elevated in quiet ecstacy, lifted into the fringes of the eternal, we simply celebrate this great visitation with rhapsodies of love, confessing that if we could praise him unceasingly for a thousand ages we could not give proper utterance to the joy which his presence is giving us in this very moment.

LIGHT FROM THE DEEPS BELOW

As we are exulting in the warm presence of the Holy Spirit in our heart, we are suddenly startled once again by a new development. Instantly, we become aware of a diminutive but brilliant glow somewhere far away from us, yet paradoxically within ourselves. A luminous pinpoint, as it were, has formed and we can scarcely plot its coordinates on the grid of our existence. This pinpoint begins to shine with a sharp brilliance, one brighter than any light we have ever known. It is clearly within us, but at depths we have never begun to imagine. It is both within us and beyond us, beyond us not in terms of height but rather in depth. It is clearly below our being, yet contained within it. It illuminates both for us and in us these measureless depths we did not previously know existed. Thus we discover another dimension of the eternal space within us.

The luminous pinpoint sparkles in the vast measureless depths that have this curious double character — within us and yet beyond our being. It is clearly a spiritual light and as soon as it is recognized, it begins to increase in its intensity. As it does so, it seems to come with steady ascent toward our being and, then, in an effortless surge it crosses the threshold and enters our being from below. No longer do we comprehend it as below our being. It is now very clearly within us, but we know it has come from unfathomable depths below us, but which are nevertheless still ours.

The Holy Spirit has quietly remained in the heart, powerfully irradiant and full of sparkling vitality. His presence causes the heart to overflow with quiet inner praise to the Lord God. The luminous pinpoint, having entered our being from below, is proceeding so to speak "upward," being drawn toward the heart where the Holy Spirit is revealing himself in glorious arrays of light.

The Holy Spirit is not marking time as he waits. While he is waiting, he is stirring up more joy and praise than we ever supposed ourselves capable of experiencing.

We have the distinct and definite feeling that this is not so much our experience as it is the Lord's. It is not so much happening *to* us as it is happening *in* us. We sense ourselves as a theatre for this divine self-experience, an arena in which God's self-experience takes place with a complexity we cannot describe.

We experience a very deep sense of appreciation at being chosen as the locale, as the theatre for God's self-experience. The common music of our familiar hymns and sacred songs fills our awareness and becomes grand symphonies of heavenly harmonies. We ourselves are being transfigured in the process. As the Lord, God the Father, Son and Holy Spirit is climbing within us to yet unrevealed heights.

All the while the ecstacy is mounting every higher, but it is a quiet inner ecstacy. The mind is in placid disengagement. Occasionally, in an objective moment it registers a thought — a sense of wonder, but generally it is caught up in the celebration to such an extent that it is in happy surrender. The body seems strangely alive. One would have thought it would have been virtually abandoned. Instead, muscles are alive with steady power. After initial pounding of the heart, it now seems to purr quietly like a well designed machine. The emotions swell with praise. In no sense do we lose identity of body or soul. We are ourselves. Although the Lord has made us into a spiritual Jacob's ladder, he does not absorb us or annihilate our selfhood.

As the divine presence so overwhelms us it is as if we had been with him from that moment described by the phrase "In the beginning God...." We are, therefore, present at Creation! Our Creation. We are present at the Crucifixion! Our Crucifixion. We are present at the Resurrection! Our Resurrection. "Holy, holy, holy, is the Lord of hosts: the whole earth is full of his glory" (Isaiah 6:3), we exclaim with the cherubim and seraphim. Yet there is no terror, no forbidding awe! No blinding holiness! It is love, and light and unsurpassed joy!

Sin has long since been confessed during the preliminary stages of the episode. The soul has been cleaned by earlier repentance, and there is no great sense of guilt. This freedom from guilt is obtained through faith in the Cross. We have believed this: "if we walk in the light, as he is in the light, we have fellowship one with another, and the blood of Jesus Christ his Son cleanseth us from all sin" (I John 1:7). Absence of sin is not a condition for his visitation, only forgiveness. Previous confession and repentance has obtained forgiveness and there is no hindrance to the ecstacy. Sin is forgiven, being nailed to the tree!

In his graciousness, the Lord grants us a moment to rest. Then an unexpected thing happens. The light from below and the joy in the heart have fused in a holy union and now a seeming new reality consisting of light/joy is formed and begins a whole new episode! We had not expected this! We thought the experience would be finished when the Light from below reached the heart. But now, this! What will it mean? What is going to happen?

A new ascent begins from the heart. A momentary concern runs through the mind which is suddenly objective enough to be concerned. This concern is that our chest cavity might not be able to contain this expanding light/joy. Surely our chest will burst! Surely our hearts will explode! This concern abates as the ascent gets under way. We are amazed at the elasticity, the expandability and resiliance of the eternal space within us. Beside this, instantly upon our sense of concern there had come the consoling solution — we find ourselves quite willing to die of an exploded heart rather than hinder this ascent of light/joy, which is Christ in us, the hope of glory!

JOURNEY TO THE HEIGHTS ABOVE THE HEART

Brilliance and ecstacy, the brightest light and the purest joy are united and have created a new dimension that can be described only as light/joy. But now, after having penetrated the lower boundaries of our being, and joining the joy in the heart, this luminous presence, no longer a pinpoint, now united with joy is now flooding the whole soul. It is no longer containable, no longer localized, but now totally pervasive, drenching the total self with joy, light and power. Every nook and cranny of the soul is filled and our total organism quietly but fully is alive with doxology and praise to God.

Having broken into the heart itself, the presence from below moves upward with forceful deliberateness. Like a slow but invincible wave it pulsates with power as it overwhelms the heart. After having crossed the boundary between the ageless, endless deeps below us, Christ has risen into our being, totally captivating it.

Now he is proposing to move *beyond* the heart itself. Before he does so, however, he builds a firm foundation in the heart from which he will journey to heavenly regions far beyond us, and take us with him.

As he begins to make preparation to go beyond the heart, we are concerned again that our heart may fail under the expansive pressure of this presence which produces such intense light/joy. The chest seems incapable of containing such a reality. In the next moment, we lose all concern for life. We desire only to experience whatever else there is to come. No longer concerned for life, we resolve to receive all that God wills to give us.

The holy presence, the full Godhead, Father, Son and Holy Spirit without distinction, continues to probe, surging over the heart with giant but gentle swells like breakers of the ocean on the shore. He fills every dimension of the heart, moving us to tears with warm and touching power. He is completely irresistable now. But we have not wanted to resist him at any point. From the very moment of being "slapped by an angel" any tendency toward resistance was overcome with only total submission and inexpressible ecstacy remaining.

As the divine presence fills the heart, there is new aliveness everywhere. The body powers seem heightened, the mind rushes with silent affirmations of praise, the emotions are quiet and steady with rejoicing in glad songs of surrender and consecration.

Gratitude radiates through the soul, marveling at having been chosen to experience in our own spiritual faculties this resurrection with Christ. Wonder, gladness and awe mingled with humility fill our consciousness. We are both humbled and honored at being so blessed in being the theatre for the divine drama. Powerful prayers of celebration, holy resolve and total surrender fill the soul. All fear subsides. The strength of the Eternal is granted in precious promises intimated to us without words. Light/joy is joined by all these other eternal resources and all are blended into a splendid symphony as the harmonies of the eternal realm ring through whatever being and existence we have expanding it and consecrating it.

Then, as if the highest peak has been scaled, the divine climber begins his descent. The recessional begins as light/joy begins to fade producing feelings of both relief and sorrow — relief that the intensity of the presence has lessened with the realization that our hearts are not going to burst after all. We feel sorrow at the thought that the episode may be ending. But the journey is not yet finished. We are delighted as the surge of light/joy begins to advance again. An altogether more powerful upward thrust is felt. This time it reaches a higher level than before. The heart sings, the mind is strangely calm, the body is alive with a soaring vitality which infinitely exceeds all the previous apexes. After reaching a higher level than the previous surge, the light/joy of his presence recedes slightly, only to thrust upward to a new height.

Again and again the process is repeated. With each new surge, greater and greater heights are achieved. With ever intensifying glory surge follows surge. The chest seems quite capable of bursting at the apex of each new thrust upward. Yet every stage immeasurably higher than the previous one is easily accommodated with ease as the divine light/joy reaches ever higher. Each time one is convinced that surely there can be no further advances. But after fully pervading the heart, we find the light/joy/power of the rising Lord proposing to go further. As with the disciples on the Emmaus Road "he made as though he would have gone further" (Luke 24:28b). And further he goes.

Finally with the surest deliberateness and undeviating purposiveness, in the greatest of surge all, the divine visitor, who is yet a permanent resident of our lives, surpasses the heart. Beyond the heart he has most certainly gone, traversing holy, heavenly places yet still somehow he is within us. We have been transported to heavenly realms above and beyond, yet we are still within ourselves, yet far beyond where we have ever been before. We are both out of the body and in it. We are both on earth and in heaven. We are both in time and in eternity. We are both in God, and have God in us. We are both alive and dead. We are both in total surrender and in spiritual affirmation. We are empty of ourselves, void of all desire, all self-assertion, all self-interest. We are full of him who fills with the fullness of the all in all. We are truly made to sit together in heavenly places in Christ, caught up in the seventh heaven. We have joined with the Psalmist who cried, "O taste and see that the Lord is good" (Psalm 34:8).

Then the recessional begins. Not all at once does he go. Without doubt that would destroy us totally. Having been filled with such fullness, we could not bear instant emptiness. As he has ascended higher and higher by effortless degrees, in the same manner does he accomplish his recessional. The waves of light/joy continue to pulsate with slow, certain rhythms. But the apex of each wave is lower than the last one. Then at last we feel him return to the deeps both below and yet remain in the soul.

When the episode finally ends, the mind is left calm and chaste. The heart is warm and yielded. The emotions are relaxed with a sense of well being and blessedness. The conviction is firm and unmoveable that Christ has risen in the soul in a previously unknown, yet anticipated way — anticipated by every spiritual feeling we have ever had, each of which is a prototype and promise of glory such as this. We have been called to unheard of newness, to unwavering consecration, to service unto death. Then we are glad.

Everything is eternally different. New dimensions of redeemed existence have been added to us and we are with him now and forever and all is well. He has taken us with him into the heavenly places, and having dwelt there for a moment or an hour, we can never be the same again.

On the first occasion of this experience, the author of this book consecrated himself to the Christian ministry. He knew nothing more than that the Lord had visited him in a special way, calling him to a calling he had recently begun to anticipate.

From the many subsequent occurrences of this same experience, he has derived comfort, assurance, direction, challenge and sometimes judgment. But always the occasion of this heavenly pilgrimmage, this being called to traverse heavenly places in Christ, has come with the greatest profundity and the most thrilling spiritual sweetness and the purest joy conceivable.

If we understand the Biblical revelation at all, we must conclude that Jesus could not be with us in our redemption, unless he had been with us previously in our creation; he could not be with us in our experience of salvation if he had not been with us in our experience as human. He could not be with us individually, if he had not been with us collectively as the whole human family. He could not be with us specifically unless he had been with us universally. This prior presence of Christ, the agent and instrument of creation, which is the presupposition of the indwelling through faith we have discussed so far, will be looked at more specifically in the next two chapters, after which we will examine the historic redemptive work of Christ which makes his presence a saving one in which we can and do rejoice.

CHAPTER 4

The Capacity to Contain the Divine Presence

Before Christ could dwell in the human heart, a human heart or soul had to be created. In creating the human, the Lord God prepared for himself a habitation on earth. He had expressed his intention to do so which Isaiah was privileged to hear: "For thus saith the high and lofty One that inhabiteth eternity, whose name is Holy: I dwell in the high and holy place, with him also that is of a contrite and humble spirit..." (Isaiah 57:15a). He therefore created the human person capable of containing the divine presence. This quality — the capacity to contain the eternal presence — is the one quality which forever distinguishes between the human creature and the other orders of creation. Nothing can diminish this delineating frontier. The capacity to extend internal hospitality to the victorious Christ of the Cross and Empty Tomb was built into the human soul from the beginning. In fact, this capacity is also the ground and source of humanness itself. Only the human can be indwelt by the Spirit of God and, as a correlate of this, every human has the full and undiminished capacity to contain him. Those who "repent and believe the gospel" (Mark 1:15) are given this privilege of being the host of Jesus Christ, the locale of his continuing residence on earth.

Preceding the indwelling of Christ given in the salvation experience is a universal, divine presence given in the creative act which produces the human as such. This is first referred to in Genesis 2:7:

> And the Lord God formed man of the dust of the ground, and breathed into his nostrils the breath of life; and man became a living soul.

To the clay figure, well formed but still lifeless, God added a portion of His own life, represented as God's breath or "wind." Wedded irrevocably to the clay figure, this breath of God created then and there the special life of man which made him a living soul.

This breath or "wind" of God, permanently given, makes the clay figure alive both psychically and spiritually. In this account, the Genesis writer conveys the thought that it is God's breath which constitutes humanness. The other orders of creation do not receive the divine presence as an inner and abiding spirit. Receiving this life of God, the clay figure becomes a living personality.

Upon this gift of the breath of God, man's own self and soul is built. The breath of God makes man human, not divine. He does not become God, even though his life is derived from the life of God. God's life alone, permanently shared with the clay figure, could make it into a human personality, a soul. So God, desiring a friend with whom he could have fellowship, gave his breath to the clay figure and it became a living, human soul. Now there were other persons beside God in the world.

The gift of his own life in the creation of the human is completely different from the gift of life God gave to all other parts of his creation. The plants and animals are alive with life created by His command, but their life is externally given. Their life does not involve the gift of God's own life. Brought into existence by his decree, externally given, they go on their way to do his will through a more or less mechanical process.

But with the human, life is given internally by the indwelling of God's own life, symbolized as his breath. The human's unique role and status in creation is based on this special relationship with God. The human being shares God's life. Man alone has God's own presence dwelling in him. Man alone has God as the ground of his being and the source of soul through an internal abiding of the divine life.

Being a soul, man has a special kind of life. No other thing can feel so deeply, think so profoundly, suffer so terribly, long so wistfully, or aspire so persistently. Nothing else in God's creation can rise so high or sink so low. Nothing else can know such forbidding grief or become ecstatic with such an earth transcending joy.

This special kind of life has its highest expression in man's longing for redemption and in the capacity to be saved. It gives him the ability to hear a word from God and to respond to it in faith. We may go even further —this special kind of life gives man the *right* to hear the Gospel. This puts a new urgency in Jesus' Great Commission to us. Being a soul, man has both the capacity and the right to hear the gospel of Christ.

In the act of blowing his breath in the clay figure, God created a creature capable of containing the living, saving presence. When he had finished his rigorous historical work of being crucified for sin and his triumphant work of rising from the dead, Jesus Christ the Savior would have a place of abode in all the earth. He would have a dwelling place already prepared.

Therefore, the soul-creating, life-granting breath, spirit or word of God creates the habitation within the human life in which Christ would dwell in due season. The pre-existing and Eternal Son, as the agent of creation, creates his own earthly dwelling-place in the hearts of men. When these hearts or souls would be opened through repentance and faith, he would gladly and gloriously enter after he had been to Calvary.

The most comprehensive name for this universal divine presence in man which creates him as human is "word." In the Hebrew of the Old Testament, it is "*dabhar*;" in the Greek of the New Testament it is "*Logos*." Thus, it is the word of God, pre-existing and eternal, the essential ingredient of mankind, the ontological word which constitutes man as such, given in the act of creation which makes man "human." This gracious gift of creation creates something capable of being saved because it makes every human heart capable of containing the historical saving word, Jesus Christ after he had completed his earthly ministry.

Thus, the word (*dabhar* and *Logos*) had been given to us in creation so that we could contain him in his salvation. Because he first gave us the word to make us human, God could later give us the crucified and risen word to make us Christians.

The creative act, therefore, precedes the saving act. Without the universal, human-creating indwelling of God's universal presence given with the blowing of his breath into the clay figure, Jesus Christ the Savior could have no habitation within us. We would be no more capable than any other animal creature of containing him as a living, saving Lord if we had not received this life of God as an ontological gift. Of course, every human person has received this gift and consequently has the capacity to receive the indwelling Savior, Jesus Christ.

THE BREATH OF GOD AND HUMAN UNDERSTANDING

The Genesis writer has received the revelation that the breath of God constitutes the human soul as a living soul. Job continues the vision by receiving the message that "...it is the spirit in a man, the breath of the Almighty, that makes him understand" (Job 32:8 RSV).

The divine breath not only gives the status of personality but also constitutes the dynamic operations of the soul. The human faculties of intelligence and understanding are seen as the products of the divine creative indwelling. We have used the term "creation indwelling" to emphasize that it is the divine breath which *creates* the human as such. The divine breath and the human personality are related as cause and effect; the giving of the divine breath and the coming into existence of the personality occur at the same time as a simultaneous action. Occasionally we have used the term "ontological presence" to describe this act by which the human as human was created. By this we simply mean that this indwelling of the divine presence is what creates the very being of the soul, what gives existence to the human personality as such. Ontology is the "science of being." Ontological indwelling is the act by which human existence is brought into being.

This breath of the Almighty gives "understanding." This is a broad term which undoubtedly refers to the entire range of human faculties, both mental and emotional as well as spiritual. The breath of the Almighty might be seen here like electricity. Moving through a complex of wires, electricity produces a great variety of results — lighting a darkened city, turning the great engines of industry, animating a still landscape with instant activity. So the breath of the

Almighty electrifies and energizes the empty forms of the human. In fact, it makes the human come alive as human. Before the breath of the Almighty was given, there could be no humanness. The existence of the human came into actuality at exactly the same moment God's breath was given as an ontological gift.

This "understanding" of man includes his self-consciousness. It is self-consciousness that distinguishes him from other things God created. Animals have consciousness, but apparently not self-consciousness. Self-consciousness requires another with whom conversation can be held. Our self-consciousness is derived from internal conversation with God in his indwelling presence. Giving his breath to the human, God is carrying on an inward conversation, an internal dialogue with his creature. This inward conversation with the present God is what gives the human self-consciousness. Without this inward conversation man would be little different from other animals. He could never be human without this breath of the Almighty.

All persons therefore, even those who scorn the Lord, owe their entire existence as human to him. This indwelling is a vast preparation of the entire human race for the possibility of the indwelling of Christ after he has completed his historical redemptive work. Thus, man is uniquely made for the gospel. The human race only is specifically created for saving grace which Christ will freely offer in the fullness of time.

The creative indwelling of God's breath has made us human and therefore capable of hearing and believing the gospel. The redemptive indwelling of Christ is its fulfillment. Just as the Holy Spirit has been given to all Christians as the "earnest" of redemption, so the indwelling creative spirit or breath has been given to all *humans* as the earnest of creation which guarantees that they *can* be saved. This earnest of creation forever reserves a place in the Kingdom of God for all who will eventually bow the knee before Jesus Christ as Lord.

THE CANDLE OF THE LORD

"The spirit of man is the candle of the Lord," (Proverbs 20:27). Once again, we must be sure that we understand just what the Biblical writer is intending to convey. He is surely affirming that the human spirit as such is the Lord's candle. The light that shines through this human spirit, any human spirit, is God's light. It is a universal ministry of which the writer speaks. Not a ministry based on willingness or intention, not a ministry contingent upon acceptance of a call or the practice of faith. Every human person, whether he will or no, is the candle of the Lord. The Lord's being and personality shines, to some degree, through the spirit of every human person as such.

This shining light of God is the essential quality of the human spirit. It is this capacity to reflect the Eternal One which constitutes the human's existence. This is what we have previously referred to as God's creation presence, or "ontological" presence, indicating that this is the one indispensible quality which constitutes the human as human. We might have called it God's "constituting" presence, for without it, there would be no human life in the world.

God willed that every human spirit should be his candle so that his light would shine in every corner of creation where any human being was to be found. This universal witness has, of course, been diminished by sin. One might almost have grounds to hold that it has disappeared altogether in lives which seem totally darkened and devastated by sin. But this light of the soul could not be totally diminished without destroying the humanness of the sinful person at the same time as its departure.

This capacity to shine with divine life is the presupposition of salvation. It is the ground of the possibility for Jesus Christ to indwell our hearts through the Holy Spirit when we have received him in repentance and faith. It is the "earnest of creation" which reserves a place in God's Kingdom for every person. One only has to turn to Christ in faith to claim this reservation. But without this original endowment with capacity to reflect God, man could never come to the one who is the light of the world, manifested in historical time and space as the man of Nazareth, the carpenter of Galilee.

THE WORD (LOGOS) IN CREATION BEFORE HE BECAME FLESH

In the Fourth Gospel the Apostle John presents us with an all-encompassing vision of the eternal status of Jesus Christ. He simply said, "In the beginning was the Word, and the Word was with God and the Word was God" (John 1:1). Taking us back to the Absolute Beginning before all beginnings, John begins where Genesis begins but adds a new thing — that which is accomplished in creation is accomplished in, through, and for Jesus Christ. In the Genesis account, Jesus Christ the Son had remained unidentified as such, but now he is acknowledged as not only agency of creation, but the eternal Word who is personal and in eternal companionship with God with whom he shares identity in some unexplained way.

John's adaptation and use of the ancient and honored *Logos* concept was determined, not by metaphysical concerns, but by evangelistic and missionary concerns. For when John beheld the Greek multitudes who needed to know what he knew, believe what he believed, to behold what he had beheld — "the glory of the only Begotten of the Father, full of grace and truth," he hesitated not for a moment, not for an instant, in doing what needed to be done — he made a radical move to express Jesus Christ in his saving power in concept and language his audience could readily understand. He simply wedded Greek form and Hebrew content. He took the *Logos* concept of Greek thought as developed primarily by Heraclitus and the Stoics, the content and meaning of which was vague and variable, and gave it specific and fixed content from the Old Testament, primarily the word (*dabhar*) and wisdom (*sophia*) of God so active and alive to do God's bidding in the revelation of God in Israel's experience. Jesus Christ is the word, the *Logos* of God, John proclaimed, and he has become flesh and dwelt among us. And there he stands!

The wisdom of this strategic move is so impressive as to its effects that one is surely justified in believing that John acted on the basis of divine revelation in his use of the Greek concept of *Logos*. That is to say, it was God's will that Hebrew wine should have been poured into the Greek vessel. And when the Hebrew experience reached its zenith, culminating in the coming of Jesus Christ, the long awaited coming one, the living water would be served in cups of Greek manufacture and the living bread presented on trays formed in Athenian foundries. The interpretation of Jesus by means of the *Logos* concept was, without a doubt, done under the direction of the Holy Spirit.

The *Logos* concept of a pre-existing, all-powerful creative force or word was ideally suited for evangelistic purposes in terms of its acceptability to the Greeks. This acceptability was based on an intellectual attraction to the idea of such a *Logos* or word active in human life and history. Apparently, it was the form only, virtually without content, which so attracted the Greeks. This Greek conception was surely a divinely created instrument to be used at the right moment. It was a part of the "fullness of time" just as much as was the Roman political domination and the universality of Greek language. In the meantime, since its content was so fluid that its meaning could vary so widely as to make it materially useless, the Greeks used it for this purpose and that, keeping it alive against the day when it would be brought to its true function, and utilized in the ministry for which it was created. John is the instrument by which the vast step is made — moving from practically empty conceptual form to a reality made alive by him who fills all in all.

"And the word (*Logos*) was made flesh and dwelt among us, (and we beheld his glory, the glory as of the only begotten of the Father, full of grace and truth)." Now we have it — the joining of the eternal and the historical in one person. And there *He* stands — eternal word and historical Jesus, the basis of the history and the hope of glory, source of redemption and ground of all reality, before our eyes — Jesus Christ, the Word and the Saviour.

The most complete picture in the Bible of Jesus' work before he was born in a manger, before he became one of us, therefore is found in John 1:1-10. In the Prologue to his gospel, John gives us insights into the ministry of Jesus while he was still in the heavenly realm with his Father. Through the Holy Spirit's inspiration, John very slightly pulls back the sacred curtain and gives us a rare glimpse of the pre-existing Christ in his ministry to the human person. John is chosen by God to show us the word (*Logos*) *before* he became flesh!

Two verses in the Prologue speak directly to Jesus' role in the creation of the human person. They are as follows:

"In him was life; and the life was the light of men" (verse 4).

"That was the true Light, which lighteth every man that cometh into the world" (verse 9).

In both verses, "men" is being spoken of in the sense of "all men," including all people everywhere, every person, the human community as a whole.

What is the significance of this? Simply that John is referring to the creative act of Christ through which the human being as such was created. It is Jesus' light, given while he was yet with the Father, that illumines the human consciousness. John is not referring to Jesus here as the Redeemer, but as the Creator. "All things were made by him; and without him was not anything made that was made" (verse 3). And how does he create the human being? John tells us. He creates the human by giving it some of his life which became "the light of men" (verse 4), and by lighting "every man" with the true Light (verse 9). By sharing his own life, Jesus gave the light of human consciousness, or a soul, to man.

Verse 9 underscores that it is "every man" who receives this light. "That was the true Light which lighteth every man that cometh into the world." Note the phrase "which lighteth every man." From this we may understand that there is not to be found in all of God's creation a single person who has not and does not to this day receive this divine, true Light. It is given to every person in the act of creation.

If John were referring to the light of salvation, he would be implying that all men are saved. But clearly, the light he is referring to is not the light of Christ in redemption, but the light of Christ in Creation. Salvation is not given to "every man" as an automatic gift. But this light to which John refers in the Prologue is an automatic gift. The only condition for receiving it is to be born as a human being.

The gift of salvation must be deliberately and consciously received. Nothing is more clear in the Bible than this — that to repent and believe the gospel is the way to receive salvation. This being the case, verses 4 and 9 cannot refer to the light of salvation. Why do we say this? Simply because the light referred to is given to "every man," all people. It is a universal gift, belonging to the human as such; it is a possession which belongs to every one simply by virtue of his being created as human. This is certain proof that John is not referring to salvation which is given only to those who "repent and believe the gospel."

So, obviously this presence John refers to is "ontological," that is, the creative presence of the Eternal Word (*Logos*) who would later be Jesus of Nazareth. This ontological presence of the word does not make us Christians; it makes us human beings. It does not save us; it creates us as human beings capable of being saved. It does not give us loving hearts as such; it gives us human hearts. It does not cause us to be born anew; it gives us birth as human in the first instance. It does not bring about the new creation in Jesus Christ; it is a necessary element of our creation as human beings. It is the light that makes the human a living soul.

Not the light of conscience, but rather the light of consciousness, not the light of love, but rather the light of life, is this Jesus Christ who eternally was before he became a man. Not a religious presence in the usual sense, but the universally spiritual, is this eternal *Logos*

— this Eternal Word. He gave himself in the act of creation so that God might have a special family on earth with whom he would have a unique relationship, knowing full well that such a family would cause him immeasurable suffering. Yet God could see the joy beyond the sorrow.

CHAPTER 5

God Through All and God In You All

Having discussed both the indwelling of Christ through faith and the creative indwelling of the breath of God or the *Logos* in chapters one through four, we come now to relate these two dimensions of human existence and Christian existence. The Apostle Paul provides, as he so often does, a succinct passage which will serve as a basis for setting forth this relationship. "There is," he says, "...one God and Father of all, Who is above all and through all, and in you all" (Ephesians 4:4a,6).

The transcendant God, exalted in majesty and holiness is truly "above all." There is maintained "an infinite qualitative difference," to use the idea of Soren Kierkegaard, between God and man. But not content to remain in majestic aloneness, God creates an order of being, the human, through which he shares himself universally, abiding in every human soul as we have seen. This is "God Through All." Later, in the fullness of time, God will step into the stream of history and enter a special relationship with certain of his human creatures based on historical redemptive acts which he himself will perform in the midst of human life. Based on repentance and faith freely chosen, this relationship is described by Paul's phrase, "God in You All." The "you" is very crucial in that it distinguishes between those who have God's ontological presence only (the natural man, those who have humanness only) and those who have added to this human endowment the saving presence of Christ and are therefore Christians (the new creation in Christ Jesus, the new humanity, the Redeemed). God Through All creates the human; God in You All creates the Christian.

GOD THROUGH ALL

God Through All is manifested as the source of all the diverse capabilities and vitalities of the soul or personality. This universal presence is the source of the rational faculties and moral conviction, aesthetic appreciation, feeling and emotions. Again, like electricity moving through wires and turning engines, lighting filaments and manifesting itself in dynamic production of motion, God Through All surges through the otherwise empty forms of the human person, empowering the psychological mechanism of the self and giving vitality even to the physical frame as well.

God Through All is expressed in creaturely love, the impulses toward natural goodness and fellow feelings of sympathy and kinship with all other human beings. It is the source of the universally human, the bond of unity that binds all human beings together in an exclusive oneness shared with no other element of the created order. This presence lifts the vision in high aspiration and inspires awe by revealing the inestimable depths upon which being itself is built. It expresses itself in a diversity of ways in human functioning — now through the intellect utilizing the brain and that invisible miracle, the mind, and again through the intuition, by-passing the complex structures of self, functioning in a direct and immediate manner. It provides the possibility of the tragic which belongs to the human alone in all of God's creation. In this experience of the tragic, man's kinship with God is very pronounced. Only God Himself and man among his creation experiences the tragic. God's ontological presence in man as the ground of the self is the basis of the tragic in man.

The ability to suffer the pangs of self-consciousness, the silent force of the human will, the possibility of having hurt feelings and grief, as well as the highest joy and happiness and all other capacities of the human personality are derived from this presence of God Through All. The individual self is formed by collecting individual experience of its own which is grounded on this ontological foundation, God Through All. In short, human consciousness with its enormous God-like mystery, so wholly distinct from all non-human life, with its pathos and pain, is the result of God's gift of humanness by means of his presence through all.

Although God Through All is the presence that creates something in need of saving, something capable of being saved, that is, the human, this presence is not a saving presence. One cannot at this present juncture of human history, in this present spiritual situation, be saved from within by the ontological presence, by God Through All. Sin has precluded this possibility. The Fall has continued to prevent that eventuality.

The Disturbing Call and the Possibility of Salvation

From this ontological indwelling, a certain natural knowledge of God can be derived but it often proves to be knowledge of a disturbing kind. At other times it manifests itself as the testimony of natural joy. When it comes as an insistent disturbance, as the disturbance of moral consciousness from which a sense of real longing for fulfillment and completion arises, it is accompanied by feelings of guilt, fear and anxiety which accompany the unanswered inward call to man. The call is unanswered because of the impediment of sin which through man's Fall, has replaced the aliveness and creativeness of spirit with the deadness of a mere static existing.

This disturbance, however, is the preparation of the soil which produces the success of the evangelistic and missionary enterprise. God Through All is the presupposition of salvation, that is to say, being human is the one and only prerequisite of salvation. Every human being is in "soteriological jeopardy," that is, under the constant threat and possibility of being saved. God's being there within every soul ontologically, as its source and ground of existence, creates the genuine and authentic possibility, full of powerful straining toward realization, that every person can be saved. In giving his breath, his *Logos* or word, as the ground of the soul, God has made a down payment, an irrevocable deposit, upon the salvation of every human being. When he blew his breath into him, God created the human capable of being saved. Because of this original creative act he is "not willing that any should perish, but that all should come to repentance," (II Peter 3:9).

The basis of soteriological jeopardy is simply to be human. Operationally, soteriological jeopardy is the inner lure of the eternal which is in every human person adhering to the ground of the soul. To be in jeopardy of redemption is a dimension of existence as human. Without this quality of constant susceptibility to salvation implanted in the human on the sixth day of creation, the experience of redeeming grace would be wholly external, dependent upon the convincing power of the human witness and subject to intellectual distortions. But the soteriological jeopardy in which every person stands assures that salvation is an inner miracle, realigning the very being of the person, fulfilling an ontological thirst so deep that it is beyond the reach even of ourselves. These deeps cry out for fulfillment. These deeps are the source of the unrest, the longing and the ultimate rest to which Augustine referred when he prayed, "Thou has made us for Thyself, and our hearts are restless until they find their rest in Thee."

That every person by virtue of being human is in soteriological jeopardy makes the work of witness a very promising work, a work already half accomplished by the creative act of the sixth day. It is not a matter of "persuasive words of wisdom," but rather "demonstration of the power and spirit" by telling the historical story of Jesus and sharing what he has done for us to cause us to be included in the community of the Redeemed.

When soteriological jeopardy is intensified by confrontation with the Christ of the gospels, the most far-reaching fulfillment is about to take place. Through repentance and faith, salvation is accomplished. Not only is there rejoicing in heaven when one sinner repents, but there is an unheard of transaction occurring on earth as the Eternal Word, the ontological ground of the soul is joined with the Saving Word, the reigning Christ, the Lord, the victorious redeemer. Then God is truly all in all in one local expression in that one saved person's life, as the deeps within him are embraced by the deeps in Jesus Christ the Savior.

This entire saving transaction is possible because of the previously granted, universally given grace of the sixth day, the creation grace which creates humanness as such.

Brief, Bright Moments When We Feel at One

Often this creative light of God is experienced as natural joy. In those seeming automatic movements of the soul through which, for an all too brief moment, it apprehends its truest nature and stands at last upon its firmest ground, we are graciously given an unfailing testimony that the breath of God is in us. When in the midst of life's confusions, we feel "at one" with ourselves, "at one" with the highest in the universe, and "at one" with the Lord, we are hearing a faithful witness who cannot purjure itself that the Eternal Word (*Logos*) is in us.

Such experience has been described by poets. For Robert Browning, it consisted of

> moments,
> Sure tho' seldom,........
> When the spirit's true endowments
> Stand out plainly from its false ones—
>
> (quoted in Harry Emerson Fosdick, *Riverside Sermons*, p. 10).

For Sarah Teasdale, such an affirmative experience was inspired by the hearing of a wood thrush at dusk in which, she says, "I snatched life back against by breast, and kissed it, scars and all" (quoted in Elizabeth Gray Vining, *The World in Tune*, p. 31).

For the philosopher, Ludwig Wittgenstein, it expressed itself in different garb. He described such a moment of well-being like this:

> ...I wonder at the existence of the world. And I am then inclined to use such phrases as "How extraordinary that anything should exist!" or "How extraordinary that the

world should exist!"
>(Norman Malcolm, *Ludwig Wittgenstein, A Memoir*, p. 70).

And more to the point of the experience we are describing, Wittgenstein reported that he often had "the experience of feeling *absolutely* safe. I mean the state of mind in which one is inclined to say 'I am safe, nothing can injure me whatever happens' " (*Ibid.* p. 70).

This sense of being "at one" does not belong only to poets and philosophers. Every person surely has on occasions, for no explainable reason, a sense of well-being. There is a sense of "rightness" to life. All the diverse and often contradictory strands of our life seem to fit together with a strange and wonderful coherence that had been previously absent.

These are the moments when such a prayer as that of Socrates is answered:

> O Lord, give me beauty in the
> inner soul,
> And may the outward man
> and the inward man
> be at one!

Such moments of experienced wholeness are the gracious gifts of God. They belong, not just to the Christian but to the entire human family as such. God is the creator of the personality, the author of the soul. For the Christian, they are gracious granting of reassurance and consolation. They are certain assurances that Jesus Christ is with us.

They are also given to the human being as such, even to those who do not know Christ as Lord. Such experience reveals something of the wonder of the soul; it tells something about the wondrous manner in which we are made. It testifies to the universal presence of

Christ the *Logos* (eternal Word) who is the ground of the creation of the human self and the source of its continued existence. Christ has a universal role in God's creation. Christ is present in a certain sense in every human soul whether Christian or not. He is with the human creature as such.

Even those who do not acknowledge him in salvation through repentance and faith are totally dependent on him for their daily life and breath. The Apostle Paul acknowledged this universal relationship to God as he preached at Athens. "For in him we live, and move, and have our being; as certain of your own poets have said, For we are also his offspring" (Acts 17:28 KJV).

The Lord has made the human being in such a way that he can be saved. Creation is therefore a part of salvation. If he had not made us like he did, he could not save us like he does. These quick bright moments of being "at one" are a call from Christ the Creator to repent and accept Christ the Redeemer. They are God's reaching to the soul, but from within, saying "Come to the One who is sending you this message." They are God's advertisements, advertisements through creation for Christ the Redeemer who has worked for us on the Cross and in the Resurrection.

The Right to Hear the Gospel

The indwelling *Logos*, God Through All, gives every person the right to hear the gospel of Jesus Christ preached. This right, adhering to the human person as such, is just as non-negotiable as his value as a human being and just as freestanding and impregnable as his dignity. Along with the absolute value of one's life there is a correlate — the absolute right to hear the gospel of Jesus Christ.

This right, like human value, however, does not belong to us because of anything we have done, but only because of what God has done. Because he has created us the way he did, he can save us like he does by dwelling within the soul from the sixth day of creation. He can dwell in us savingly after he had completed his redemptive work. Just as the creative presence of the *Logos* dwells in us to make us "living souls," so the redeeming presence of the crucified and risen Savior dwells in us to make us Christians. In his creative act, God has given us the "earnest of creation," by which he guarantees the possibility (but not, of course, the actuality) of every person's being redeemed.

On the basis of the creative act of God, every person has this inalienable right to hear the Gospel and therefore to possibly come to saving knowledge of the *Logos* who became flesh and dwelt among us. Because God has already laid the foundation for salvation (by making us living souls), it is God himself who expects those he has previously chosen to be Christians to proclaim the gospel to all the others. Since God has made every person capable of being saved, it is reasonable for him to expect those already saved to carry the saving message to the rest.

The evangelistic and missionary obligation, then is grounded in the very structure of God's creation as well as in the Cross and Resurrection of Jesus Christ. To fail in this missionary commission is not only to violate the clear command of Christ, but also to fly in the face of creation, and to repudiate the creative fiat of God given when he blew his breath in the clay figure he had made. When he blew his own breath into the figure, he then and there gave the creature the non-compromisable right to hear the rest of the story, to hear about the finished product, to know what he had done to bring this creative work to completion. "For he is not willing that any should perish, but that all should come to repentance" (II Peter 3:9).

Wherever there is a human being, this the gospel must be preached. Having received the divine breath, the human soul becomes a veritable vortex of swirling powers which draw, as it were, the gospel to it. What God has joined together, let no man separate. The human soul and the gospel are made for each other. None has the right to infringe upon this privilege every person as person has. This right to hear what Jesus Christ did for us during his earthly sojourn is non-negotiable and beyond all compromise.

Although the special call to ministry and mission is very personal and individual, the ultimate call is in the creation act of God in which he gave his *Logos* to be the constitutive indwelling presence which makes the human a living soul. Because of God's commitment in creation, all Christians must labor mightily to bear witness of the gospel to every human being. Not based on our feelings, our being "under obligation both to Greeks and barbarians, both to the wise and to the foolish" (Romans 1:14 RSV) is finally based on the creative act of God in which he gave to every person the inalienable right to hear the gospel when he made him a living soul.

Service to God and Service to Neighbor

The indwelling *Logos*, God Through All, residing in every human soul makes service to God and service to neighbor one and the same thing. Indeed, there is no obligation for service to God required in the Bible which cannot be fulfilled totally in service to our neighbor.

God Through All and God In You All

The parable of the sheep and goats (Matthew 25:31-46) makes this identification very specific and shockingly clear. When the King comes he will say to those on his right (the sheep),

> "Come...inherit the kingdom...For I was hungry and you gave me food, I was thirsty and you gave me drink, I was a stranger and you welcomed me, I was naked and you clothed me, I was sick and you visited me, I was in prison and you came to me." (verse 34-35)

The righteous are very surprised to hear this and inquire when all this took place. To their denial that they had done all this service to him, Jesus replies, "Truly, I say to you, as you did it to the least of these my brethren, you did it to me" (verse 40). Then the King brings the charge against the unrighteous, "You saw me in need and did not serve me." When, when? is the fevered reply, "when did we see you in need and not minister to you?" The reply of the King is simply the opposite side of his response to the righteous. "Truly, I say to you, as you did it *not* to one of the least of these, you did it not to *me*" (verse 45).

Surely it is the kinship between God and his children created by the indwelling *Logos* that makes this identity of service both possible and necessary. When God put himself in the soul of the human he created a non-negotiable value, an inalienable right to dignity to every person and, at the same time, made every human being the object of his undying love. "For God so loved the world..." (John 3:16).

This kinship between God and the human being is the ontological basis for all social action and not only Christian social ethics but "human" social ethics as well. The dignity of the human cannot be abridged. It is absolute, free-standing, and dependent on nothing that can be compromised. The absolute value of the soul is the one recognized absolute in all the world. Although it has been violated, even on a vast scale as in the Nazi atrocities against the Jews, such violations are considered abhorrent, perhaps even by the perpetrators themselves except in the actual moments of madness produced by whatever demons that possessed them.

Jesus clearly set the standard; he clearly affirmed the non-negotiable, non-instrumental value of the human being. Walter Rauschenbusch, writing finely of Jesus' absolute love for people, declares:

> The God of Jesus was the great Father who lets his light shine on the just and the unjust, and offers forgiveness and love to all. Jesus lived in the spiritual atmosphere of that faith. Consequently, he saw men from that point of view. They were to him children of God. Even the lowliest was high. The light that shone on him from the face of God shed a splendor on the prosaic ranks of men. (*The Social Principles of Jesus*, p. 9)

Joyce Proctor Beamon, a well known North Carolina novelist, remarked poignantly to columnist Dennis Rogers,

> Human life is sacred...And anytime you can do something good for another human being, you have touched their soul. When you do that, you have dealt with the heart of God. You have touched eternity.
> (*News and Observer*, December 7, 1982)

How like Jesus! "Truly, I say to you, as you did it to one of the least of these my brethren, you did it to me." And the converse is true — neglect in serving others is neglect in serving Christ.

In this we see the immanence of God in its most practical expression. He has put himself right down here among us so that we may locally serve the eternal. This is a gracious act on God's part — putting himself among us in every human soul so that we may serve him without leaving home, as it were. Every human person, including ourselves, then is a conduit for service for God and the only conduit. "If any one says 'I love God,' and hates his brother, he is a liar" (I John 4:20 RSV).

The creative act of God on which this identity of service of God and service to neighbor is based is the granting of the eternal *Logos* the pre-existent Son and Word to be the foundation of the human soul. The life of God is in every person. "...the Lord God formed man of dust from the ground, and breathed into his nostrils the breath of life; and man became a living being (soul)" (Genesis 2:7 RSV).

FROM GOD THROUGH ALL TO GOD IN YOU ALL

The light of human consciousness derived from God Through All, from God's universal giving of himself to create the soul, has not been without tragic darkening. It has been ravaged by an aggressive and powerful force. The entrance of sin and death into human experience meant that the light could no longer shine from within in its full brilliance. The fellowship could not continue in its original clarity. The intended grace of creation was repudiated by man's willful disobedience. The *Logos* was prevented by man's choice of sin from accomplishing what he longed to accomplish by this universal indwelling the heart of men. But it was not destroyed. It continued to create humanness, to activate the reason, the emotions, the entire inner life of man, both psychological and spiritual. Although "...the Lord was sorry that he made man on the earth, and it grieved him to his heart" (Genesis 6:6 RSV), his love for Noah kept him from destroying what he had created. So God willed man's continuation as man.

But God would not fail. In the fullness of time, therefore, he must make a radical move; he must perform a daring act. He would step into the stream of human experience himself, not as an outsider, not as an observer, but as a fully participating human being. In this coming, he would remove the impediment of sin, knowing full well that it meant the Cross. Nevertheless, he would be incarnated as Jesus Christ.

As the Word made flesh, God appears in the stream of human events — to Abraham, Moses, Isaiah. He appears to kings, priests, shepherds, common folk in the ordinary walks of life. God appears in their historical situation. The entire historical revelation in both the Old and New Testaments has as its subject this appearing of God in human history. The one who is the ground of human experience as such, the creator of human existence through the blowing of his breath, comes into human experience as Jesus of Nazareth. God Through All is offering himself to every person through Jesus the Christ so that by our choice, by repentance and faith, he might become God in *you* All to us. The universally shared God Through All is the presupposition of the personally and individually chosen presence through the Cross and Resurrection which creates us as Christian believers, as the new humanity.

So when the fullness of time came, when everything was ready, the Eternal Son, the *Logos* (Word) of God, stepped forth into the world as a human person. Taking upon himself the physical body and the personality of a human being, appearing as Jesus of Nazareth, he began the short but momentous sojourn that would complete the work begun in creation when God shared his own life with the clay figure he had made. So, as John tells us, "The Word (*Logos*) was made flesh, and dwelt among us, (and we beheld his glory, the glory as of the only begotten of the Father), full of grace and truth" (John 1:14).

CHAPTER 6

The Eternal Word Steps Forth

This is how it happened. One cold, clear star-filled night, the Eternal Word became flesh through the womb of a woman. He was born right here, and in a manger at that. As a man, he dwelt among us all — the rich and the poor, the high and the low. He came to those who were seeking him in constant scanning the heavens for evidence of his appearing, as well as to those who would hide from him when he came. He came to those who would reach out for the hem of his garment as well as to those who would reach for spikes for his hands and feet. He became flesh to dwell among us all. And because he was pleased to dwell among us, he would finally dwell within us after he finished his sojourn here.

On this particular night, when the fullness of time was come, "God sent forth his Son, made of a woman, made under the law, to redeem them that were under the law, that we might receive the adoption as sons" (Galatians 4:4). Although this lowly event seemed trivial from the human point of view, apparently it was understood differently from the eternal point of view since it was accompanied by heaven-sent cosmic phenomena and visitors from the realms of glory.

When God began to open the windows of grace in this fulfillment of his ancient promises, symphonies of angelic hosts were heard like none human ears had ever heard before.

As shepherds watched their flocks by night, they were surrounded by heavenly choirs singing, "Glory to God in the Highest and on earth peace, good will to men." As others were drawn into the drama, they began to sing as had Mary in her magnificent doxologies when she first saw her blessed cousin Elizabeth, after the Annunciation of the Angel.

The aged prophet Simeon, after waiting a lifetime for the consolation of Israel, saw the infant Jesus and proclaimed in the musical cadences of an overflowing soul that his reason for living had been fulfilled. Then he asked that he might now be let go in peace for at last as he said, "...mine eyes have seen thy salvation" (Luke 2:30). How could this aged witness have said what he said in any other mode except that of singing melody?

Anna the prophetess, also waiting to be a witness, could scarcely have prevented herself from breaking into ecstatic song as she beheld the prince of peace, the Redeemer-King quite asleep in his mother's arms.

Luke emphasized that the coming of Jesus produced music in many hearts. Carefully, he records the symphony of the soul that is produced by the appearing of the Lord. There is music in the person of Jesus — the music of the eternal glory, the music of the heavenly spheres, the music of forgiveness of sin, the music of life overcoming death, the music of redemption and restoration of original sonship to God.

At the time before his birth, the songs of Israel had died down. The joy of heart had fallen to a low ebb. Like a receding tide it had left the faith of Israel as forlorn as empty shells along the shore. Lifeless, prosaic language and the dry technicalities of the hair-splitting literalists had replaced the rhythms of poetry and the power of song of the prophets and psalmists. But Jesus restored singing to the soul. When he came, the world could sing again!

As he came in a glorious burst of music, so does he make the soul sing with his saving approach, with his redemptive coming even in these days. As he brought life again to poor tragic Israel, so does he bring life again to dry, dead souls and make them sing today.

After proper praise and exuberant joy at this ultimate coming of God in Christ, after the recognition of Jesus by devotee and would-be destroyer alike, after appropriate religious ceremony in recognition of the vast significance of what had happened, the music subsides, angel choruses make their way back to the other side of the division between heaven and earth. The singing is over temporarily and the work of preparation begins. Luke tells us of a calm normalcy being restored in order to allow the child to grow and wax strong, to become filled with wisdom and to receive the continuing grace of God upon him (Luke 2:40).

"And the word was made flesh and dwelt among us, (and we beheld his glory, the glory as of the only begotten of the Father, full of grace and truth)." And there *He* stands — Eternal Word and historical Jesus, the basis of the history and the hope of glory, source of redemption and ground of all reality, before our eyes — Jesus Christ, the Word and the Saviour.

The Eternal Word became flesh and dwelt among us in time and place and we like they of long ago have beheld his glory and proclaim that it is the glory of the only begotten of the Father, full of grace and truth. This is the central affirmation of the Christian faith celebrated in hymn, scripture, and prayer — that the

Eternal Word, the Son everlasting, has clothed himself in human flesh, being born of woman and has come here where we are to live the perfect life, to reveal the full glory of God and to give his life on the Cross of Calvary in an agonizing redemptive death but then to rise as the victor from the dark domain, and that his name is Jesus Christ.

He who knew no sin, would be made sin for us.

He who owed no debt to death, would allow himself to be overwhelmed by the last enemy in order to make it just that.

He who was and is eternal, free from every limitation, would place himself in the bondage of this world's time and place for us.

This is the essence of the gospel — that into this realm of the temporal the eternal is breaking. This is being accomplished now as then by the appearing of the man Jesus Christ. Through this Carpenter of Nazareth, the eternal order is constantly invading these fleeting scenes of time and space. Through the life of this traveling preacher, a power from the dimension beyond has come into our dimension. The eternal Son came here wearing the garb of a man, actually becoming a human being, risking everything in identifying himself with flesh and blood. In doing so he formed a bond that shall not be broken throughout the endless reaches of the aeons that are before us. Jesus Christ is his name.

We hear nothing more until he is twelve. The incident in the temple on the trip to Jerusalem in which he amazes the doctors of the law with his questions and answers assures us that the preparation is still coming along.

From that episode in the temple until he is about thirty years of age, the years have been silent ones. The sound of music, long ago subsided, is replaced by a strange seriousness on the countenance of the young man from Galilee. The whole world would soon see the reason for the singing at his coming three decades before.

And then, as with a terrible swift sword, with staccato movement, as if the whole forces of heaven and earth had joined together for some valiant and heroic occurrence (which of course they had), the young carpenter steps forth — out of obscurity into the limelight, out of tranquility into a heart-piercing turmoil.

A voice cries in the wilderness to announce that the curtain of the ages has been drawn.

The man steps forth to be baptized and receives the dramatic endorsement of the Father as the Holy Spirit descends upon him to remain.

An amazing ministry of compassion is begun. A message of redemption sounds forth. Overwhelming resistance is met as the powers and principalities come with relentless power. Yet never has so serene a life been lived before.

Then he is crucified — two thieves and a soldier understand for the first time who he is, and who they are.

After that a grave breaks open — a shroud is found neatly folded. A profound silence pervades the scene. Out of the hush of the garden the risen Lord addresses his disciples. They run to tell the others and to tell the world.

Jesus Christ the *Logos* has stepped forth and continues to step forth. He has drawn near and continues to draw near.

His glory has been revealed and continues to be revealed to those who seek him. And sometimes to those who do not. Once that glory is seen, it transforms the beholder! And he meets us along life's way.

When Jesus meets us along the way, the whole reality of the human and the heavenly stands embodied; the eternal and the historical are revealed wholly in him. Because he is the *Logos* who was breathed into our souls at creation, we recognize him instantly as our eternal contemporary, as our friend from the beginning of life itself. When the veil is lifted from our eyes, we are amazed that we could ever have considered him a stranger! Jesus has never been a stranger to anyone. When he is introduced in historical revelation by preaching and witness, through faith we recognize him as the deepest thing in *us* standing there before us. Then and there, we recognize that the one who was called "the Stranger of Galilee" was not and never has been a stranger to us, or to anyone.

When we meet him along life's way and surrender to him as Lord, the deepest deeps in us, long yearning for fulfillment, long calling out with urgent hungering and thirsting for satisfaction, finally recognize and embrace the deepest thing in him. The crucified and risen Lord, the victor over sin and death is what our deepest souls have longed for, begged for, wept for. And there it is — it is Jesus Christ! The deeps within us, of which he is the author, embrace the deeps in him, made manifest on the Cross and in the Empty Tomb, and we reach a self-realization we never dreamed possible!

CHAPTER 7

The Cross and the Atoning Sacrifice

The atoning work of Jesus Christ the *Logos* is the miracle of miracles. The most immediate miraculous dimension of it is that the followers of Jesus, after some initial baffled confusion at the turn of events, saw beyond the surface meanings of it and intuitively understood, without theological reflection or philosophical analysis, that this strange gruesome event was a manifestation of the *love* of God.

In the night they saw the dawn of day.

In unimaginable disaster they saw inconceiveable victory.

In the shaking of the foundations, they found the Rock that does not move.

In the seeming triumph of the force of death, they saw the opening of the fountain of endless life.

In the heavy silence of the shrouds of grief, they heard Hallelujah Choruses such as even Handel could not compose.

In the fulfillment of the promise of the ages, they saw the fellowship of the dead great and small standing before God.

They comprehended the incomprehensible, heard the inaudible, viewed the invisible and saw with newly opened eyes the supposed victim become the victor.

While blood was flowing, flies were swarming, soldiers were cursing, crowds were jeering, dice were rolling, while Jesus Christ himself writhed in agony with his side slashed and body broken, they began to see the love of God. So they reported. So they believed. So they knew. They made this interpretation so dominant that it has never been effectively questioned, much less refuted. Through thick and thin, the vision has held strong. In cooler times with the opportunity for reflection, the vision has not faded under the scholar's labors. The cynic's assault has been turned away from the gate again and again by this truth breaking through into his jaded awareness and embracing him, the cynic. The prayer of the half-believing believer has been answered to his surprise when God has indeed shown him his love beaming through the Cross.

It would take considerably more reflection, more pondering over scripture, more brooding in prayer, however, to discern the miracle going on in the realm of the eternal —

> the condemning of sin by God through the lifting up of Jesus;
>
> the washing as white as snow of that which had been red like crimson;
>
> the utter defeat of the power of the prince of the air and the triumph over the principalities of evil;
>
> the breaking of the hold of cancelled sin and the setting of prisoners free;
>
> the completed reality of forgiveness now instantly available to those who could trust him with childlike faith;

The Cross and the Atoning Sacrifice

the passing over by death of all those who would display the blood of the Lamb eternally slain;

the new song of victory sung by the angels in glory which could now be sung by the Lord's redeemed.

It is all there on the Cross on that bleak hill far away, outside Jerusalem's walls, the power and the promise available to all who would receive it and sufficient for all who would believe it to avail to them a city whose builder and maker is God.

The subject of the atonement is a sacred and serious subject before which we stand as on holy ground and it is appropriate that we remove every shoe that might profane this sacred mystery. Here we must speak with the ultimate hush of awe and reverence as we stand before the Cross of Jesus Christ and attempt to interpret what happened there.

Therefore we need not expect common human understanding to grasp it, or the power of the natural reason to embrace it. Common ways of knowing do not apply, nor can the eyes of the flesh see what they saw, nor mere human ears hear what they heard. The object to be known, the Cross with Jesus the Eternal Word nailed to it, requires a new way of knowing, a new epistemology, the epistemology of the spirit. This spiritual way of knowing is referred to in I Corinthians 2:10-16.

The Roman centurion who, perhaps well ahead of Jesus' entourage, confessed at the crucifixion, "Surely this man was the Son of God" (Matthew 27:54b) led the way in the experience of the miracle of spiritual knowing. Then Jesus' own inner circle began to interpret what happened on Golgotha as the love of God being manifested in this event like it had never been manifested before. The ability to see and interpret the Cross in this way, against all empirical data, is in itself a miracle. The spiritual eyes of the soul had been opened by God himself who never leaves himself without a multitude of witnesses.

Until atonement was made for sin so that the human heart could become an acceptable habitation for Christ, he could not dwell there. His work of atonement was a prerequisite for his indwelling. Sin must be dislodged before he can enter to dwell. The seriousness of sin is seen in its power to prevent Christ's entrance into the heart and thereby keeping the saving works he has come to perform from being applied. The blood of the Cross is not on us until Christ is in us. Whatever denies the Lord admission and continuing residence in the heart is the vilest of sins. Shallow views of Christ in his atoning work probably derive from shallow views of sin. Atonement must be made before the redemptive plan could culminate in the indwelling of Christ, its fullest expression. So he set his face steadfastly toward Jerusalem and shouldered the Cross.

When he finally cried out just before he gave up the ghost, "It is finished," he had to wait only for his sure and certain Resurrection and the eventual sending of the Comforter before he could take up his residence in the hearts of those who would receive him through repentance and faith.

So grand and comprehensive is Isaiah's vision of the coming Redeeming One, God's Suffering Servant, that it refers not only to a glorious future but also reaches back to the pre-existing savior who has born our sins as long as sin has been a part of human experience — to "the lamb slain before the foundation of the world" (Revelation 13:8b).

> He is despised and rejected of man; a man of sorrows and acquainted with grief:
>
> And we hid as it were our own faces from him; he was despised and we esteemed him not.

The Cross and the Atoning Sacrifice

> Surely he hath borne our griefs, and carried our sorrows: yet we did esteem him stricken, smitten of God, and afflicted.
>
> But he was wounded for our transgressions, he was bruised for our iniquities: the chastisement of our peace was upon him: and with his stripes we are healed.
>
> All we like sheep have gone astray; we have turned everyone to his own way: and the Lord hath laid on him the iniquity of us all. (Isaiah 53:3-6).

God has been laying human sin upon him since the first occasion of sin. As the *Logos*, Jesus Christ, has been suffering for these sins while holding them in his own person preparing to make atonement for them through his suffering once and for all when he came into the world. Dwelling in us individually as the creative ground of the personality, the Eternal Christ received every blow that sin could inflict. The laying of our iniquity upon him is in the very order of creation. Thus the atoning work of Jesus, although it reaches its apex in the historical Cross of Calvary, has been in effectual progress since the first act of disobedience. Since man's first rejection of immediate fellowship with God in preference for his own independent history, this atoning work has been in progress. The dubious freedom asserted by man to choose his own history and to endeavor to be his own lord, subjected the Lord of Glory to age long suffering both while he was in the eternal realm and in shameful, pitiful agony and death in the world of time and place.

Had not Jesus been the *Logos*, the agent and ground of creation, he could not have had our sins laid on him prior to his coming here. And it would not have been possible for him to be the Redeemer. As the *Logos*, he had been suffering for sin ever since sin began. This is the meaning of John's vision of Christ as "the Lamb slain from the foundation of the world" in Revelation. Ever since the beginning of the rule of death and darkness, ever since the beginning of the reign of the powers and principalities with spiritual wickedness rampant in high places, Jesus the *Logos* has born the suffering of man's sin. As the ground of creation, Jesus has always been bearing man's sin in his own person, even before the incarnation, even before the Cross.

But even the suffering of Jesus in the eternal realm, before he came to earth, before he went to the Cross, as intense and powerful as it must have been, could not atone for human sin. As shocking and outrageous as is the thought of the suffering of the divine, and this in his own heavenly sphere, yet heavenly suffering alone could not atone for our sin if we understand the Biblical revelation at all.

Since suffering in eternity involved only the suffering of God, it was not sufficient. To be effective the atonement must involve the ultimate degree of suffering — it must involve the crushing of the human as well as the crushing of the divine. Atonement therefore could not be accomplished wholly and exclusively within the eternal realm. It must occur in that locality where the human as well as the divine could experience the ultimate tragedy. It must take place within the human realm as well as the divine. It must take place in the temporal dimension as well as the eternal. And the place so chosen by circumstances from the human side and by eternal decree from God's side was the Cross of Calvary. In the crushing of the heart of Jesus the divine and the human suffer the ultimate suffering. Jesus pathetically confessed, "My soul is exceeding sorrowful into death:..." (Mark 14:34b). The events of the Passion were the beginning of the human suffering parallel to that of the divine already long in progress. And when he cried from the Cross, "It is finished" (John 19:30), the ultimate suffering which could only be human and divine together was completed. With the shedding of his blood unto death and the surrendering his life, human and divine, the atonement was now complete.

The ultimate solution therefore had to be a divine/human sacrifice accomplished in the human realm. A human sacrifice was not enough; a divine sacrifice only would not suffice. It had to be a divine/human sacrifice, or a godly sacrifice in the authentically human realm. So the Eternal Word took upon himself our humanity. He became a man in order that the human might bear suffering parallel to that of the divine. On the Cross Jesus suffered total death — death in the human realm and death in the divine. The pre-incarnational suffering was brought to its effective conclusion on the Cross. Just as he had suffered in the eternal realm, so he has now suffered in the temporal. Just as he had suffered in his divinity, so has he now suffered in his humanity — death in human and death in the divine. Then and there was the atonement completed. Then and there sin and death were dealt with once and for all.

That Jesus suffered for sins for ages before his actual physical birth into the human family does not in any way lessen the historical actuality of the Cross or its gruesome reality. The historical actuality of the crucifixion of Jesus on Golgotha must never be called in question. In a time which can be fixed on a calendar and a place which can be located on a map, Jesus Christ went forth bearing his Cross and was crucified. Then and there he died. But this could be effective for our redemption only because he had already been suffering for our sins before he came here. His suffering in eternity could not redeem us, but without it his suffering on the Cross could not have done so either.

Rather than Christ's suffering for sin in the eternal realm compromising the historical validity of his work on the earthly Cross, it is the necessary pre-requisite which makes the work on the Cross effective. If Christ had not been suffering *there* for sin ever since it began, the Cross could have meant nothing *here*. Without his bearing our sin ever since sin began, the Cross would have been a dark and tragic illusion, an empty cistern bearing no water of life.

This person who stands before us in historical garb is also the Eternal Word who is the ground of the soul given in creation. At a time which can be set in a historical context and in a place that can be found on a map this person Jesus Christ went forth bearing his Cross and was crucified. He went to Calvary to complete his work begun in heaven, in eternity, when at the beginning of sin he began to bear it in his own person and suffer for it.

So he was led to the place of the skull called Calvary. Without what he had always been doing long before he came to earth as a human, what he did on the Cross would have been only a tragic miscarriage of justice; the pathetic death of a good man which accomplished nothing.

What he was doing on the Cross, therefore, was completing the work of suffering begun in eternity. Since he had been collecting all human experience, including that which was reprehensible and repulsive to him, that is, sin, he could die the atoning death on the Cross, a universal death, death in the eternal and death in the historical. Only total death, death of the human and death of the divine could atone for our sin.

Leading Biblical texts concerning the atonement require so much more than the idea of mechanical substitution. Isaiah 53 and Romans 6:5-11, for instance, require so much more than simply Christ being substituted mechanically for the sinner while the sinner stands aside almost as a spectator. In such passages, the concept of the actual identification of the Redeemer and the redeemed, the Atoner and the atoned is so overwhelming that we must go well beyond the notion of substitution in our interpretation of the atonement.

Our union with Christ through mutual indwelling ("...ye in me, and I in you" John 14:20), gives us an identification with him more intense than human minds can conceive. Through this identification, Christ died *for* me, but not as my substitute, rather as *myself*. Christ's death is *my* death. Christ's identification with us is so real that our sins in the process have become his. Therefore, Jesus, although sinless himself, has taken our sins so thoroughly upon himself, that they have become his. If he has made our sins his *own*, then they are his. These sins were ours, but they became his. The identification between Christ and the sinner is so thorough-going that we cannot say otherwise.

Our sins become his sins and his death becomes our death — "Ye are dead and your life is hid with Christ in God" (Col. 3:3). The identification is now a completed transaction. If our sins are not his, his death could not be ours.

Many interpretations of the atonement fail at the point noted in Anselm's reply to Boso, "You have not as yet estimated the great burden of sin" (*Cur Deus Homo*, chapter XXI, tr. by S. N. Deane, in *St. Anselm: Basic Writings*, LaSalle, Ill.: Open Court Publishing Co., 1961). Christ is often thought of as aloof from the sin he would atone, as unaffected by the weight and burden of them. But as the pre-existent ground of the soul on whom all sin was laid we see the dreadful weight Christ bore as he made our sins his, really his.

Because he emptied himself, "...we see Jesus, who was made a little lower than the angels for the suffering of death, crowned with glory and honor, that he by the grace of God should taste death for every man" (Hebrews 2:9). What dreadful weight he bore when "the Lord laid on him the iniquity of us all" (Isaiah 53:6b) but we rejoice in such costly grace.

CHAPTER 8

Victor From the Dark Domain

What marvels lay behind the statement in Luke 24:3: "And they entered in (the tomb) and found *not* the body of the Lord Jesus." Because they did not find him in the grave, they could truly call him "Lord," this time with a new conviction and in an unprecedented daring of faith. He was and is the Lord indeed because, "When they sought him among the dead he could not be found; when they looked for him in the tomb he was not there."

Ever since it became apparent that he would not be found, doxology has been pouring from Christian lips. Words of praise and wonder from the elegant, "Worthy is the Lamb that was slain to receive power, and riches, and wisdom, and strength, and glory, and blessing" (Revelation 5:12) to the commonplace Easter hymn, "He arose, he arose, hallelujah, Christ arose," have been sung, preached, and published to the ends of the earth. Those who sat in darkness have seen a great light. "Through the tender mercy of our God: whereby the dayspring from on high hath visited us" (Luke 1:78).

The resurrection of Jesus has no precedent, no natural antecedents, and stands completely beyond the categories of scientific knowledge. Occurring on the very boundary between time and eternity, it happened both within history and beyond it. It is living, eternal history in the midst of the stream of passing time.

Unlike Lazarus (John 11) who was called back to this earthly life where he would have to face death again, Jesus passed completely through death and came out on the "other side." In doing so, he tore away the chains of sin and death and made available to those who would believe a completely new kind of life, both in this world and in the eternal order.

Neither Lazarus' experience nor any other human experience could offer a parallel to the resurrection of Jesus. There is no prior example. Human power could neither produce it nor prevent it. It was the miracle of miracles! Therefore, doxology is the media which best communicates its truth and mediates its power. Thus, we open our hearts and proclaim:

> Low in the grave he lay, Jesus my Saviour!
> Waiting the coming day, Jesus my Lord!
>
> Up from the grave He arose,
> With a mighty triumph o'er his foes
> He arose a victor from the dark domain,
> And He lives forever with His saints to reign.
> He arose! He arose! Hallelujah! Christ arose!
> (Robert Lowery, "Low In The Grave He Lay")

> When they sought him among the dead,
>   He could not be found;
> When they looked for him in the tomb,
>   He was not there.

"And they entered in and found *not* the body of the Lord Jesus." This miraculous occurrance in the grave is a bright shining light in a world of dark death. It is the freedom of grace and truth in the midst of bondage to distortion and lies. It is the permanently abiding invitation to us to sit together in heavenly places in Christ Jesus while we walk through the earthly time and space God has granted us. Through his resurrection truly, "...the dayspring from on high hath visited us" (Luke 1:78 KJV).

THE RESURRECTION OF JESUS IS A PRESENT REALITY

Through the indwelling of the risen Savior, his resurrection, like his death, is a living experience, a historical-spiritual reality that becomes a part of our own lives. Neither as lifeless pageantry, nor empty parody, nor powerless imitation does it enter into our experience. But the Resurrection, like the Cross, is experienced first hand when the one to whom both happened comes through our repentance and faith, to dwell within us. These momentous events are so vividly reenacted in us when he takes up residence in our hearts that it can be said that we have died with him in his death and have risen with him in his Resurrection.

The unique and uncanny power of these very historical events to become mysteriously present realities in our contemporary religious experience is not in the events themselves. They have been brought into our lives by Christ's coming to dwell there. As the Spirit ministers Christ's indwelling to us, the limitations of time and place are totally overcome and we know them as living, saving events.

In his role as the promised Comforter, the Holy Spirit accomplishes his work by calling the Cross and Resurrection of Jesus to our remembrance and revealing their meaning and power to us over and over in our spiritual pilgrimmage.

Every spiritual experience, from the charming warmth of the heart felt in public worship to the overwhelming confrontation with Christ which requires a total redirection of life, is simply some aspect of the Holy Spirit's administration of the living Christ in us in a moment of special blessing. Since Christ dwells in us, we have died with him and been raised with him once and for all. Our salvation is finished and complete. But it pleases God to bless us over and over again through a spiritual reenactment of his redemption of us. All worship, therefore, is participating again in his redemptive sacrifice and victory over death. The sacrifice is not being repeated however. Repetition is neither possible nor necessary since "...this man, after he had offered one sacrifice for sins for ever, sat down on the right hand of God" (Hebrews 10:12 KJV). Only the subjective counterpart is being repeated.

This subjective counterpart of his death and resurrection is given to us as the source of spiritual life, of encouragement, of peace, of challenge and specific callings from the Lord. The Christ who dwells in every redeemed heart rises up within us in such moments to warm our spirits, assure us, console and convict us. And although our salvation is certain from the first cry of repentance and the first affirmation of trust in Christ as Savior, this blessed repetition of the experience of his life and death within us through his indwelling is the way the Holy Spirit directs and sustains our Christian lives. The indwelling risen Christ boldly makes his presence felt within us. When he makes us know he is there in these moments, whether in ordinary worship or overwhelming spiritual experience in private, we rejoice in his reaffirmed presence.

THROUGH HIS RESURRECTION CHRIST IS LIVING FOR US

The union of the risen Christ with our own spirit is so

real that he is, in fact, living for us before the throne of God. Just as he was our representative in vicarious death, so is he our representative in vicarious life. Just as he died for us on the Cross, so does he live for us before the throne in the heavenly realm. Jesus' great statement, "I am the resurrection and the life..." reaches its full meaning in the understanding that he is our resurrection and our life in the same sense that he is our crucifixion and death. He takes our place in resurrection and life as he did in crucifixion and death. Therefore the life he lives before the throne of grace is our true life on the basis of which God relates to us, "for he is our righteousness."

We find that Paul's statement, "...for me to live is Christ..." (Philippians 1:21) to violate the very canons of language and meaning until we understand that Paul is saying that in the spiritual realm Christ is living his (Paul's) life for him.

The entire concept of the Christian's life in Christ presupposes Christ's vicarious living for us. Because he is in us, we are incorporated into his life. Justification by faith implies and requires the truth that he is our righteousness, that he is our justification. As our advocate and intercessor, he is living a perfect life for us before the throne of God obtaining daily for us God's never failing grace. Thus our salvation is a dynamic, ongoing event as Christ lives the perfect life for us before the throne. The possibility of the failure of this grace, of course, is non-existent since he lives in us and we live in him. He is therefore the "Christ who is our life".

In Ephesians 2:5-6, Paul makes it very clear that the true life of the believer is being lived on the heavenly plane in the present time, through and by Jesus Christ.

> Even when we were dead in sins, (God) hath quickened us together with Christ, (by grace are ye saved); And

hath raised us up together, and made us sit together in heavenly places in Christ Jesus.

As we sit together in heavenly places in Christ, he becomes the center of our life being lived in the heavenly sphere. Although we have not completely reached this heavenly destination, although we have not fully attained this new spiritual life in Christ, nevertheless our lives are being lived for us by him before the Father which we claim as our own through faith. He is therefore our representative in the highest life just as he was in the deepest death.

The passage which speaks of this vicarious life most startlingly is Colossians 3:1-4:

> If ye then be risen with Christ, seek those things which are above, where Christ sitteth on the right hand of God. Set your affections on things above, not on things on earth. For ye are dead, and your life is hid with Christ in God. When Christ, who is our life, shall appear, then shall ye also appear with him in glory.

In harmony with many other affirmations of the same truth, here Paul refers to the fact that the believer is "risen with Christ." But he goes well beyond previous statements to affirm Christ's vicarious living for us with the otherwise enigmatic statement that "...ye are dead, and your life is hid with Christ in God."

It is now "Christ who is our life" and not we ourselves. When this "Christ, who is our life" appears in glory at the end of the age, he will present to the Father this life he has been living for us in the place of the fragmentary life we have been living day to day in the world. The righteousness of Christ has become ours through his dwelling in us and our concurrent dwelling in him.

The life he lives for us is the model that draws us toward greater consecration and realization of the Christlike life. His representative living for us is the spiritual power which makes us free to live more as he lived, to walk more as he walked. Rather than detract from the obligation to attain qualitative excellence in our present life, Christ's vicarious living for us constantly draws us to greater and greater consecration. His life for us not only gives us a model to endeavor toward but also provides the power that enables us to attain more completely the ideal of Christlikeness. This drawing power continues throughout life.

> I am crucified with Christ: nevertheless I live; yet not I, but Christ liveth in me: and the life which I now live in the flesh I live by the faith of the Son of God, who loved me, and gave himself for me. (Galatians 2:20)

Because he lives our true life for us, we are free to live for him rather than for ourselves. Because he is living his life *in* us within the earthly sphere, he can and does live our lives for us in the heavenly realm. Jesus referred directly to this dual indwelling when he said, "At that day ye shall know that I am in my Father, and ye in me, and I in you" (John 14:20). "At that day" refers to the coming of the Comforter, the Holy Spirit, which occurred at Pentecost. Therefore, this mutual inherence is made known by the Spirit as he illumines and interprets both Christ in us and our dwelling in him in the heavenly realm. He is the living person and power who is both resident in our spirits and the ascended one in whom we are contained.

Both the death of Christ becomes ours and the life of Christ becomes our life, when he enters into vital union with us. When he enters our lives to reside, he brings with him and gives to us all the benefits and the reality of his Cross and Resurrection. When he gives us himself through mystically attaching himself to us, we receive everything he has accomplished in his redemptive ministry. As the Apostle Paul so dramatically puts it:

> Know ye not, that so many of us as were baptized into Jesus Christ were baptized into his death? Therefore we are buried with him by baptism into death: that like as Christ was raised up from the dead by the glory of the Father, even so we also should walk in newness of life. For if we have been planted together in the likeness of his death, we shall be also in the likeness of his resurrection. (Romans 6:3-6 KJV)

Therefore, "we are buried with him by baptism into death." Then, we are raised to "walk in newness of life" because his death and resurrection have become ours. Had he not been called from the coldness of the grave, we could never have had such a blessing. But because he lives, we live and celebrate his resurrection in the voice of singing and exultant praise.

CHAPTER 9

The Metaphysic of Consecration

"For as by one man's disobedience many were made sinners, so by one man's obedience shall many be made righteous" (Romans 5:19). In this way, the Apostle Paul presents in a succinct statement the fundamental principle of the Metaphysic of Consecration. Jesus puts it even more pointedly, indicating that the power which consecration mediates resides in him personally: "For their sake I consecrate myself" (John 17:19a). This total consecration of Jesus, even to obedience unto death on the Cross, is the only source of this world-changing power. It is "for their sake" and for the sake of all creation that creation-renewing power has been attached to the consecrated obedience of all Jesus' true disciples. To face this difficult world without this armor of God and without a power sufficient to change it would have been more than they could have endured. And more than we could have. Therefore, Jesus assigned his world-transforming power to them and us. He made it readily available to everyone, from the lowest to the highest — to all, in fact, who would surrender themselves to total consecration to his will.

Begun at Pentecost, that occasion on which the Risen and Triumphant Savior took up residence in his people's hearts, becoming the indwelling spiritual presence in and through the Holy Spirit, this irresistable power capable of changing the structure of reality surged forward until in just a few short years it was knocking on the door of Caesar's Palace in Rome.

Even now, in those all too infrequent but glorious moments, when the currents of spiritual energy surge with such forceful intensity in the local congregation that decisions for Christ as Savior and surrender of life to him becomes easy, if not irresistable, we know that the Metaphysic of Consecration and the dynamics of renewal are in operation. This rising of the tide of spiritual energy consists in the heightening of the inward spirit which guarantees the success of the proclaimed and written gospel of Jesus Christ.

All this is possible because Jesus Christ was "...found in fashion as a man, he humbled himself, and became obedient unto death, even the death of the cross" (Philippians 2:8). God the Father then acknowledged the victory he won through suffering obedience and honored him:

> Wherefore God also hath highly exalted him, and given him a name which is above every name: That at the name of Jesus every knee should bow, of things in heaven, and things in earth, and things under the earth; and that every tongue should confess that Jesus Christ is Lord, to the glory of God the Father
>
> (Philippians 2:9-11).

When every tongue has confessed that Jesus Christ is Lord, then the Metaphysic of Consecration shall have been fulfilled. When the full glory of what Jesus has done is presented to God the Father, the love that sent him to the Cross will have filled all in all.

The total consecration of Jesus himself resulting in his Cross and subsequent Resurrection was and is completely adequate to bring about this universal

The Metaphysic of Consecration

acknowledgment and confession of his Lordship of which Paul speaks. Although it has been delayed, nothing can prevent its ultimate fulfillment. The Metaphysic of Consecration activated by the "revealing of the sons of God" is the operational method by which God will bring it about (Romans 8:19-23).

Jesus' choosing his disciples is a paradigm of the Metaphysic of Consecration. He did not rest the success of the Kingdom on their specific work. Their work, like our own, was often faltering and inadequate. Except for the glowing report of the Seventy on returning from their preaching tour (Luke 10:17-18), the work of the original disciples seems to have been generally ineffective. Even the Twelve, so blessed with personal intimacy with Jesus, were more often than not caught up in bafflement and confusion, never understanding what Jesus was trying to accomplish or even who he really was. At times their trivial conversation reveals jealousy, childish self-interest and detachment from the urgency and reality of the situation before them. Again so like us, his contemporary disciples.

But Jesus called them and us to be the shock troops of the new reality. Through consecration-in-itself we would all be carriers of Jesus' ministry of renewing and restructuring the creation through the saving of every soul who would believe. He called them and us not primarily to *do*, but to *be* — to be colonies of the Eternal, outposts of the Kingdom of God in the world. First, he moved to activate the Metaphysic of Consecration through these Twelve. Afterwards, he added others —"as many as would receive him."

To have the living Christ as the indwelling Lord is to be made a bearer of this Metaphysic of Consecration. To Christians, this is not an optional question. It is necessary that everyone who professes Christ to be obedient in all things and thereby to be an agent of eternal power in the world. Because of our faith, which Christ honors and blesses through personally indwelling our hearts, we are inescapably in the vanguard of the forward march of his unresting truth.

FOUR BLESSED SEERS

Four great visionaries have seen the glorious state of creation resulting from the final realization of Christ's consecration even to the death of the Cross. One saw it as a coming glory straining to be born. Two others saw it as a distant but certain reality which would bring in a glorious new age, a wonderful new order of things, but without temporal or spatial parameters. The fourth beheld it "coming down out of heaven from God" (Revelation 21:2) at the end of the age.

First, Paul. He describes the renewal of creation as a thing straining to be born. The new order hovers on the very edge of things. It is waiting for only one thing. It "waits with eager longing the revealing of the sons of God." In a startling passage, Paul sets forth in detail that which God allows him to see.

> For the creation waits with eager longing for the revealing of the sons of God; for the creation was subjected to futility, not of its own will but by the will of him who subjected it in hope; because the creation itself will be set free from its bondage to decay and obtain the glorious liberty of the children of God. We know that the whole creation has been groaning in travail together until now; and not only the creation, but we ourselves, who have the first fruits of the Spirit, groan inwardly as we wait for adoption as sons, the redemption of our bodies. (Romans 8:19-23 RSV).

The whole creation has been groaning in travail, existing in agony, awaiting the glorious results that will

The Metaphysic of Consecration

come about with the "revealing of the sons of God." We who have received the "first fruits of the Spirit" groan with the rest of creation until it is set free from its "bondage to decay" and obtains "the glorious liberty of the children of God."

All this comes about with the "revealing of the sons of God," that is, when the people of God will begin to really activate the Metaphysic of Consecration through total obedience to the Lord. There is, of course, nothing more to be done from God's side. Everything necessary has been done. The Parable of the Great Supper indicates that everything is now ready. "Come," Jesus said, "for all things are now ready" (Luke 14:17b). All the resources necessary for the activation of the Metaphysic of Consecration are available. Only the revealing of the sons of God remains because "everything necessary has been done," as Karl Barth phrases the meaning of this Parable.

Jeremiah and Isaiah saw the fulfillment of Jesus' consecration in a different light. Whereas Paul saw the renewal of creation just about to break through, these two classical prophets from the eight century B. C. saw it as a more distant reality based in the certainty of God's covenant with Israel which he would renew and heighten. This is Jeremiah's vision:

> ...this shall be the covenant that I will make with the house of Israel: after those days, saith the Lord, I will put my law into their inward parts, and will write it in their hearts, and will be their God, and they shall be my people.
>
> And they shall teach no more every man his neighbor, and every man his brother saying Know the Lord: for they shall all know me, from the least of them unto the greatest of them, saith the Lord: for I will forgive their iniquity, and I will remember their sins no more.
>
> (Jeremiah 31:33-34)

Law stamped on inward parts! Truth written on the heart! Universal acclamation of the glory of the Lord! No need to teach — everyone already knows. "Know the Lord" is a redundant phrase.

Then, the blessed Isaiah was also chosen to receive a grand vision of this coming time.

> The wolf also shall dwell with the lamb, and the leopard shall lie down with the kid; and the calf and the young lion and the fatling together; and a little child shall lead them. And the cow and the bear shall feed; their young ones shall lie down together: and the lion shall eat straw like an ox. The suckling shall play on the hole of the asp, and the weaned child shall put his hand on the cocatrice's den. They shall not hurt nor destroy in all my holy mountain; for the earth shall be full of the knowledge of the Lord, as the waters cover the sea.
>
> (Isaiah 11:6-9)

All natural enmity is overcome. Nature itself, heretofore red in tooth and claw, is at rest with combatants previously locked in agelong struggles for survival sleeping peacefully together. So gentle has the new creation become that it is at the command of a little child. Murderous poisons are neutralized. Hurt and destruction are passed over. But the most marvelous of all is this: "...the earth shall be full of the knowledge of the Lord, as the waters cover the sea."

These two prophets seem to have beheld heavenly visions which perhaps continued to belong to the heavenly realm, but which, in their spiritual optimism and vibrancy of faith in the Lord, they seem to transpose into the earthly key. They saw a new order, a triumph of grace, but they were not given the time/space coordinants and therefore did not know where or when this grand fulfillment was to come about. They only knew that it would be unbelievably splendid! What could be more splendid than this universally possessed

The Metaphysic of Consecration

knowledge of God. "...they shall teach no more every man his neighbor, and every man his brother saying Know the Lord: for they shall all know me" (Jeremiah 31:34). "...the earth shall be full of the knowledge of the Lord, as the waters cover the sea" (Isaiah 11:9).

The prophetic vision of a totally restored creation sees the time coming when the external word of preaching and witness will not be necessary. Total spiritual inwardness will become an actuality and no longer will the outer word be needed. The dispensing with the outer word in itself signifies the ultimate miracle. This state of affairs will confirm the non-voidness of the proclaimed word and proves without a doubt that it never on any occasion returned to the Lord until it had accomplished the task to which it was sent (Isaiah 55:11). The proclaimed word has fulfilled its ultimate mission by making Christ the All-in-all. It has finally exalted his name to the one before which every knee shall bow. This is not salvation without preaching and witness. It is salvation after preaching and witness have fully accomplished their purpose of restoring spiritual inwardness on a world-wide scale.

The earthly phases of this vision which occurs on the historical plane is not conversion without the gospel. It is the inwardness of spirit raised to the extent that the preached gospel becomes immediately successful. This rising tide is accomplished by what we have called the Metaphysic of Consecration.

The restoration of creation through the revealing of the sons of God comes about through the renewal of the universal spirit in man. The *Logos*, the breath of God, given on the sixth day of creation is the ground of the human spirit as such. As the sons of God give themselves through consecration they become channels through which the grace of Jesus Christ the Crucified and Risen One flows. Then the ontological spirit in every human person in whatever place on earth is raised, creating vast possibilities for belief in the gospel and salvation of souls from within.

Apparently the privilege of fixing the temporal and spacial parameters of the final fulfillment of Christ's consecration was reserved for the fourth seer, the Apostle John. Yet the time and place are still incalculable. But clearly, John beholds the fulfillment of consecration as occurring at the transition from this age to the next. The specifics are still God's secret alone. Quite clearly, however, it occurs after the time when the hymn writer's vision has become a reality:

> And, Lord, haste the day when the faith shall be sight,
> The clouds be rolled back as a scroll,
> The trump shall resound and the Lord shall descend,
> Even so, it is well with my soul.
> (Horatio G. Spafford, "It Is Well with My Soul," Baptist Hymnal, 1956)

John's description of his own vision occurring as the clouds are "rolled back as a scroll" is sufficient:

> Then I saw a new heaven and a new earth; for the first heaven and the first earth had passed away, and the sea was no more. And I saw the holy city, new Jerusalem, coming down out of heaven from God, prepared as a bride adorned for her husband; and I heard a great voice from the throne saying, "Behold, the dwelling of God is with men. He will dwell with them, and they shall be his people, and God himself will be with them; he will wipe away every tear from their eyes, and death shall be no more, neither shall there be mourning nor crying nor pain any more, for the former things have passed away.
> (Revelation 21:1-4 RSV)

After much descriptive detail and many wonderful scenes, John's vision seems to connect very directly with that of Jeremiah and Isaiah, sharing some com-

The Metaphysic of Consecration 103

mon features, especially the fact that set forms of worship and testimony of witness are now superceded.

> And I saw no temple in the city, for its temple is the Lord God the Almighty and the Lamb. And the city has no need of sun or moon to shine upon it, for the glory of God is its light, and its lamp is the Lamb. By its light shall the nations walk; and the kings of the earth shall bring their glory into it, and its gates shall never be shut by day — and there shall be no night there; they shall bring into it the glory and the honor of the nations. But nothing unclean shall enter it, nor any one who practices abomination or falsehood, but only those who are written in the Lamb's book of life.
> (Revelation 21:22-27 RSV)

Although there are earthly features in John's vision, it seems clear that the New Jerusalem is incapable of earthly realization although there are some aspects which are capable of historical fulfillment. But finally it comes about only after the Alpha and Omega has traversed that vast distance from the Beginning to the End. The historical order is brought to a conclusion; the new order supercedes it. And the new order is brought in by the return of Christ in his long promised and eagerly awaited Second Coming. "Surely I am coming soon. Amen. Come, Lord Jesus!" (Revelation 22:20 RSV).

IN THE MEANTIME

Needless to say, the object of the four great visions has not yet been realized. But nothing can prevent its coming to pass. The reality beheld is there, in full operation and glory, on the very edge of this historical order straining to be born here. It is not as if there were some great void beyond our present age. Jesus' consecration, finished on the Cross and in the Resurrection, has assured that "everything necessary has been done." It is only a matter of mediating this reality from the heavenly realm to the historical; of transposing Christ's victory from the other side to this side. In the meantime, between the Cross and its total fulfillment in Christ's Second Coming, Christians have been made the instruments of this transposition. Christ has established the Metaphysic of Consecration through which every devout person can have a part in the coming of glory. There remains only the revealing of the sons of God who will take up the Metaphysic of Consecration with deliberateness. With intentional consecration, spiritual inwardness will rise to such a degree that those who hear the gospel can believe instantly. At preaching and personal witness, they are immediately convicted and converted without delay. Heightened inwardness creates such a longing anticipation of the gospel's being spoken and produces such an overwhelming hunger for the meat of the word, such a thirst for this water of life, that proclamation and witness are instantly accepted in repentance and belief. Then jubilant praise and exultant shouts of joy pour forth from those whose ears have now heard what their souls have been crying out for from that first moment in which a wistful sigh disturbed the quiet innocence of childhood until full-fledged conviction caused them to cry out "O wretched man that I am."

By consecrated obedience, every person who is a believing Christian, regardless of station in life, intellectual endowment, material resources, or obscurity of location and reputation, is to be a part of world-wide evangelism. Obedience to Christ raises the level of inwardness everywhere and creates the possibility of instant belief where none existed before.

Christians, therefore, must have greater devotion, deeper belief, more complete trust, and absolutely unimpaired obedience. Then the Metaphysic of Consecration will operate to change reality. It will allow flood-tides of Spirit to cascade into the dead darkness of human depths, and new creation will occur, new levels of being will be attained. Reality is changed by such radical devotion to the will of God. The real is significantly enriched by total obedience. Since it has as its object the remaking of reality itself, we call the structure through which this power flows a metaphysic because metaphysics is concerned with reality as a whole. Since its method is consecration, we have called the possibility of changing the whole of reality through obedience to Christ the Metaphysic of Consecration.

We must follow Jesus in living the Metaphysic of Consecration and thus activate the dynamics of renewal. God can do what he wants to do through either one person or a million. Sometimes he seems to prefer the one, sometimes the millions! But it is only through the practice of the Metaphysic of Consecration that the coming spiritual revolution will be brought about.

Radical consecration of even a few Christians gives the proclamation of the gospel irresistable power, while uncommitted Christians rob it of its inherent force, making its proclamation hollow and ineffective. It is time for Christians everywhere to activate the Metaphysic of Consecration so that the same sweeping, overwhelming power of the early Christian proclamation and to a lesser degree that of all subsequent spiritual movements such as the Great Awakening and the Wesleyan Movement can be experienced once again in a dark and deadly world.

"There is a tide in the affairs of men," Shakespeare observed appropriately. There are currents of possibility, waves of spirit which sweep over an era or age when great spiritual accomplishment is possible, easy, or even irresistable. There are other times when deadness and lethargy reign. What is the source of these spiritual tides? The Holy Spirit acting through the Metaphysic of Consecration! If Abraham could have found only one righteous man in Sodom, the whole of reality would have been changed. In the same manner, it is possible for one person, one family, one congregation to commit itself to Christ to the extent that tides of willingness, waves of spiritual possibility sweep the entire world. Usually, this one person, family or congregation has no inkling that it has been the instrument which activated this spiritual renewal. Because of the Metaphysic of Consecration, one person can influence the whole world.

ACTION AT A DISTANCE AND THE BODY OF CHRIST

Deep consecration performs "action at a distance." The philosopher G. W. Leibniz (born 1646) developed this concept of "action at a distance" to explain how one remote "monad" or unit of reality could influence another although separated from it. The Metaphysic of Consecration performs spiritual "action at a distance." The source of the spiritual power which is being manifested in a certain place may be at a great distance from that place and the identity of the person or persons through whom it comes may never be known. The discerning heart knows, however, that somewhere someone is engaging in the ministry of a consecrated life which is enabling this particular work.

Ordinary prayer offered for anyone other than ourselves is an example of spiritual action at a distance. Frank Laubach quotes G. Campbell Morgan who tells the story of Marianne Adlard in his book *The Practice of Prayer*. Marianne was a bedridden invalid girl in

The Metaphysic of Consecration

London who had read of Dwight L. Moody's work among the poor of Chicago. "O Lord," she prayed, "send this man to our church." In 1892 Moody took his second trip to England, not intending to do any work on that visit.

> But the pastor of Marianne's church met Moody and invited him to preach for him. Moody came, and after the service asked if anybody desired to decide for Christ. Hundreds rose to their feet. Moody was so surprised that he repeated his request more clearly, and they rose again. During the next ten days four hundred persons were received into the church. Moody told Morgan, "I wanted to know what this meant. I began making inquiries and never rested until I found a bed-ridden girl praying that God would bring me to that church. He had heard her, and brought me over four thousand miles of land and sea to her request.
>
> *Prayer: The Mightiest Force in the World* (Fleming H. Revell Company, p. 36).

Such people committed to the Metaphysic of Consecration, believing fervently that prayer and devotion changes the very structure of reality and the possibilities of life, are in the secret vanguard of the spiritual revolution the world so desperately needs and which is certainly coming. They are the true revolutionaries of the world! God will not allow the Cross and Empty Tomb to be treated the way they are treated today for an indefinite period. He is calling multitudes to activate the Metaphysic of Consecration by simple obedience to Christ and active love for him. Then the gospel will be preached with earth-shaking power even by mediocre men! The Cross and Resurrection will become invincible again!

Because Christ is the Head of the church and the church is his Body (I Cor. 12:12-31; Col. 1:18; Eph. 1:22-23), consecration acting at a distance is well grounded in scripture.

Just as in the human body, the pain of one organ can effect the comfort and health of another organ far removed from it, so can the source of spiritual blessing be far removed from where it is experienced in the spiritual Body of Christ. When well-being is restored to an injured foot, or a broken arm, the entire physical organism celebrates with rejoicing. So does the spiritual progress of one person or church spread rejoicing over the entire Body of Christ. "And whether one member suffer, all the members suffer with it; or one member be honoured, all the members rejoice with it" (I Cor. 12:26 KJV).

Whatever is occurring in the churches, whether spiritual exaltation or regression, is in fact occurring in the head of the Body, that is, in the life of Christ. Christ himself is the *locus* of the suffering or rejoicing that is appropriate to his local church. As head of the church, he distributes the results of consecration according to his infinite wisdom.

Sometimes the saints of God are perplexed by what seems to be a failure of their consecration. They need not be so. They need only to be aware of the capacity of consecration to act at a distance. It was said of Jesus, as he returned to Nazareth, "...he did not do many mighty works there, because of their unbelief" (Matthew 13:58). Mark makes the case somewhat stronger in affirming, "...he *could* do no mighty work there..." (Mark 6:5a). What happened was that Jesus' consecration was hindered in its effect. Does this mean that it accomplished nothing? Not at all. On another day and in another place the accomplishment of his consecration was applied and joyfully received. It is quite impossible for true consecration to fail in its task of changing reality through heightening inwardness. God's word never returns to him void.

The Metaphysic of Consecration

Truly dedicated ones, real practitioners of the Metaphysic of Consecration are those who are losing their lives for Christ's sake. They avoid the great peril of saving their lives for themselves only to be losing them all the while. To lose one's life for Christ's sake is to be willing for the effects of one's consecration to be manifested and utilized elsewhere.

There may be instances of spiritual growth which appears to be genuine but where there is little evidence of consecration. Often such growth and advance necessarily comes through the action of consecration at a distance. Some saint, perhaps far removed from the scene, is losing his or her life for Christ's sake. This consecration is the source of the life which is being expressed. The great Head of the Body is directing the power of consecration where it is needed most.

Jesus asked his true saints to be willing for the results of their consecration to be secretly diverted to another place, to be used somewhere else where the need was great and consecration was not being practiced. Receiving no credit or recognition from the world, the truly consecrated person is obedient to Christ's command to lose one's life for his sake.

So consecration's power is never lost. Often its effects are revealed in close proximity to where it actually occurs, but not always. The truly dedicated person must never despair on any occasion. True consecration will win the day. The highest practice of the Metaphysic of Consecration occurs when we are losing our life for Christ's sake.

We readily see how blind and foolish it is for one to boast about the success of one's own work. For a church or an individual to take credit for accomplishments is very misinformed, unspiritual and unbiblical. The pride which leads one to do so may very well be the pride that has required consecration from some distant quarter in order to avert spiritual disaster. Paul presses the lesson home to us that no Christian has any right whatever to boast since God alone is the giver of all good and spiritual gifts.

The greatest service, therefore, to both God and man is to seek deliberately God's will revealed in scripture and then to intentionally commit oneself to do it with absolute consecration. When we are willing to do so, we do not have to live on borrowed spiritual power; we do not have to import spiritual resources, but we ourselves have become channels of grace through the Metaphysic of Consecration. Our own devotedness gives impetus and heavenly power to the proclamation of the gospel if not where we are, then somewhere else where it is being spoken and read. And to some extent everywhere else in the world through the heightening of the ontological spirit. When he invited his disciples to become agents of the Kingdom through consecration, sparks were ignited and tongues of fire spread ragingly throughout the whole world as the gospel was proclaimed. In the process, the power of the Cross and Empty Tomb became living realities wherever this message was spoken. "The word is nigh thee, even in thy mouth, and in thy heart: that is, the word of faith, which we preach" (Romans 10:9 KJV).

We cannot speak it and live. Dying with Christ, we live the consecration which gives it invincible power. Living with Christ, we die and in our death to sin and self we "lay in dust life's glory dead, And from the ground there blossoms red Life that shall endless be" (George Matheson, *O Love That Wilt Not Let Me Go*, Baptist Hymnal, 1975). In being hid with Christ in God we become instruments which speed the coming day when at the Crucified One's name every knee shall bow and when at the Risen One's loving approach on every Road to Emmaus hearts everywhere will burn with tongues of unquenchable fire.

> Blessing, and honour, and glory, and power, be unto him that sitteth upon the throne, and unto the Lamb for ever and ever. (Revelation 5:12b KJV)

> Now unto the King eternal, immortal, invisible, the only wise God, be honour and glory for ever and ever. Amen. (I Timothy 1:17 KJV)

> Even so, come Lord Jesus. (Revelation 22:20b KJV)

www.ingramcontent.com/pod-product-compliance
Lightning Source LLC
Chambersburg PA
CBHW070928160426
43193CB00011B/1610